"*Thunder in the Sky* is sage advice with contemporary application for modern business people who want to understand the essence of the Chinese mind."

—Duane L. Bowans, managing director,
Americas Pacific Operations, Tektronix, Inc.

"Business people will find this valuable book worth reading again and again for its universal wisdom and subtle insights." —Al Frank, publisher, *The Prudent Speculator*

"*Thunder in the Sky* is an ancient Chinese strategy text for government, business, and war. Like Sun Tzu's *The Art of War*, which dates from the same period (700–221 B.C.), it presents terse, powerful stories and epigrams that illuminate timeless principles. . . . *Thunder in the Sky* is as effective for managing personnel as for thwarting enemies." —*Success*

"*Thunder in the Sky* provides, in short, clear lessons, insights into ourselves as leaders, as business citizens, and as human beings." —Robert V. Adams, CEO, Xerox Technology Ventures, and president, World Business Academy

# Thunder in the Sky

# ALSO BY THOMAS CLEARY

*The Japanese Art of War: Understanding the Culture of Strategy* (1991)*
*The Essential Confucius* (1992)
*The Book of Five Rings* (1993)*

## I CHING STUDIES

*The Taoist I Ching*, by Liu I-ming (1986)*
*The Buddhist I Ching*, by Chih-hsu Ou-i (1987)*
*I Ching: The Tao of Organization*, by Cheng Yi (1988)*
*I Ching: The Book of Change* (1992)*

## TAOIST STUDIES

*The Art of War*, by Sun Tzu (1988)*
*Mastering the Art of War*, by Zhuge Liang & Liu Ji (1989)*
*Back to Beginnings: Reflections on the Tao* (1990)*
*The Book of Leadership and Strategy* (1992)*
*The Essential Tao* (1992)
*Wen-tzu: Understanding the Mysteries*, by Lao-tzu (1992)*
*The Spirit of Tao* (1993)

## BUDDHIST STUDIES

*Zen Lessons: The Art of Leadership* (1989)*
*Rational Zen: The Mind of Dogen Zenji* (1993)*
*Zen Antics: One Hundred Stories of Enlightenment* (1993)*

*Published by Shambhala Publications

# Thunder in the Sky

## SECRETS ON THE ACQUISITION AND EXERCISE OF POWER

### TRANSLATED BY THOMAS CLEARY
*Foreword by Chin-Ning Chu*

*Shambhala*
*Boston & London*
*1994*

Shambhala Publications, Inc.
Horticultural Hall
300 Massachusetts Avenue
Boston, Massachusetts 02115

9  8  7  6  5  4  3  2  1

*First Paperback Edition*

Printed in the United States of America on acid-free paper ♾
Distributed in the United States by Random House, Inc.,
and in Canada by Random House of Canada Ltd

*Library of Congress Cataloging-in-Publication Data*

Thunder in the sky: secrets on the acquisition and exercise of power /
translated by Thomas Cleary; foreword by Chin-ning Chu. — 1st ed.
p.    cm.
Translation of: Kuei-ku-tzu, Tung ling chen ching.
ISBN 1-57062-027-X (pbk.)
1. Kuei-ku-tzu, 4th cent. B.C.  Kuei-ku-tzu.  2. Keng-sang, Ch'u.
Tung ling chen ching.  I. Cleary, Thomas F.,  1949– .
II. Kuei-ku-tzu, 4th cent. B.C.  Kuei-ku-tzu  English 1994.
III. Keng-sang, Ch'u. Tung ling chen ching  English 1994.
B128.K8374T3613   1994        94-9613
181'.114 — dc20          CIP

Cover art: *Dragons Painted in Ink* (detail) by Chen Rong.
Painting on silk, Song dynasty. Reproduced by
permission of the Commercial Press (Hong Kong)
Limited from *The Art of the Dragon.*

# CONTENTS

*Foreword*                                                vii
*Translator's Introduction*                                xi

THE MASTER OF DEMON VALLEY

  Opening and Closing                                  3

  Response                                             9

  Acceptance and Solidarity                           14

  Stopping Gaps                                       20

  Excitation and Arrest                               23

  Opposition and Alliance                             27

  Figuring out Psychological Conditions               30

  Pressuring                                          34

  Assessment                                          39

  Strategic Thinking                                  44

  Decision Making                                     50

  Talismanic Sayings                                  52

  Basic Course: Seven Arts of Covert
    Correspondence                                 56

  Holding the Pivot                                   70

  Course from the Center                              71

  *Notes*                                             77

THE MASTER OF THE HIDDEN STOREHOUSE

  Preserving the Way Intact                           99

  Applying the Way                                   106

CONTENTS

The Way of Government             111

The Way of Leadership             126

The Way of Administrators         131

The Way of the Wise               135

The Way of Education              142

The Way of Agriculture            150

The Way of War                    157

*vi*

# FOREWORD

IN TODAY'S DEMANDING business world the fierce game of competition has literally evolved into bloodless warfare. The result is, as the Chinese say, *"Shang chang ru zhan chang,"* or, "The marketplace is a battlefield." Although this militaristic view of business may seem novel, it isn't news to Asians, whose leaders for centuries have drawn from ancient art-of-war treatises to help them achieve and maintain power. The Asian people view success in the business world as tantamount to victory in battle, with both directly affecting the survival and well-being of their nation. Since they perceive that the true nature of business competition is that of war, they act accordingly.

Asians believe that mastering tactics and strategies is essential for success in the marketplace. Asian rulers, from ancient to modern, have always placed great importance on the study of classical Chinese treatises of subtle wisdom and strategy. These scholarly works brought great power to those who were able to apply their principles to the affairs of daily life. One of the most important principles of Asian thought is that all elements of life are interconnected, so there are no real divisions between philosophy, spirituality, the art of war, the art of acquisition, the exercise of power, and political and business affairs. The wisdom that guides the general in battle is the same wisdom by which the politician exercises power and the business person maneuvers financial advantage. Asians don't tend to find anything strange in searching a text devoted to military strategy for principles that apply to situations in the family, the work place, or the world at large.

For thousands of years, the Chinese have been observing and documenting the dynamics of life and nature. In the process they discovered a certain rhythm of universal force that is unfailing and consistent, and applicable to every aspect of life. The philosophers captured this rhythm and later taught princes and scholars how to incorporate these principles into the administration of state affairs. The ultimate goal was to achieve absolute rule over China and its subjects. This was particularly true from 700 through 221 B.C.E., when China was going through a period of weak central government and total division among all the feudal lords. Conquering was the aim, and survival was the game. Because of this chaotic environment, China became a natural incubator for some of the greatest philosophical doctrines and art-of-war treatises. Great thinkers and strategists such as Confucius, Lao-tzu, Chuang-tzu, and Sun-tzu all lived and left their marks during this period.

One of the great masterpieces of the time was called *The Master of Demon Valley* (translated here for the first time by Thomas Cleary as part of *Thunder in the Sky*). *The Master of Demon Valley* was particularly prized by Chinese scholars and power-brokers and has had profound influence on the course of Chinese history. In 221 B.C.E., using theories found in *The Master of Demon Valley*, the great Emperor Chin was able to unite China and end its prolonged five-hundred-year brutal civil war. *The Master of Demon Valley* is a work that continues to enjoy extraordinary stature in Chinese literature because of its subtle and profound wisdom. However, this book was not written for casual reading. Ancient sages and scholars often devoted their entire lives attempting to master this erudite and elusive knowledge.

It is exciting to see this great Chinese treasure (accompanied by another Taoist classic, *The Master of the Hidden Storehouse*) finally presented to Western readers. These two powerful texts have inspired emperors and strategists throughout Chinese history. Now the forces that guided the ancient emperors to victory can also navigate today's business people to profitability.

It is important to understand that the profound wisdom of China is not the property of the Chinese people but belongs to all humankind. The wisdom revealed in this book relates to experiences that all people enounter, enabling us to recognize the universality of the forces that shape our lives. In fact, the true treasure of *Thunder in the Sky* lies in its ability to uncover the mysterious relationship between spiritual insight and physical attainment.

In today's fierce domestic and international economic

warfare, it is gratifying to see that American business people will be able to study this profound Eastern wisdom—translating these theories for practical use in the day-to-day quest for a better life.

CHIN-NING CHU
President, Asian Marketing Consultants
author of *Thick Face, Black Heart,*
*The Asian Mind Game,* and
*The Chinese Mind Game*

# TRANSLATOR'S INTRODUCTION

"THUNDER IN THE SKY" is an ancient Chinese symbol for great power, meaning progress and growth, strength going into action. Understanding the development, exercise, and consequences of every kind of power is a traditional element of Chinese thought.

The original Chinese philosophy of power came from participative observation of nature, society, and the inner mind. In early times, this led to the quest for mastery of the powers in plants and metals, in order and organization, and in extra-ordinary perceptual and cognitive capacities.

As a result of this interest in the attainment, use, and abuse of power, an advanced science of human behavior was developed and employed over the course of centuries. This study of human weakness and strengths was originally carried out in a comprehensive context of moral and psychological training, but the refinement of strategic arts eventually became a specialty among some thinkers because of preoccupations with questions of power and national security.

This book presents the first English translations of two secret classics of this ancient tradition, *The Master of Demon Valley* and *The Master of the Hidden Storehouse*. Each of these texts, from its own perspective and in its own way, provides a practical course in special modes of human development and empowerment.

The first work, *The Master of Demon Valley*, is a highly controversial classic generally attributed to the Warring States period of ancient China, which began around the middle of the first millennium B.C.E. The military classic by Sun-tzu, *The Art of War*, is also from this period, as is the Taoist classic *Chuang-tzu*. Although very closely related to both these martial and Taoist traditions, *The Master of Demon Valley* is ordinarily associated with a relatively obscure school of thought known as *Tsung-heng hsueh* (*Zongheng xue*).

A number of meanings are contained within the name of this controversial school, which is generally concerned with the psychological and strategic aspects of statecraft. The surface reading of the term is "vertical and horizontal learning," which uses the names for specific geographical patterns of alliance in Warring States China to represent the science of strategic diplomacy and statecraft in a rapidly changing world.

Another way to read *tsung-heng hsueh* is as "the learning of freedom of thought and action." This refers to the ability to evade imprisonment by the forces of conventions and pressures of events, while nevertheless retaining the capacity to interact meaningfully and effectively with the world at large. In strategic terms, this aspect of the science is defined as learning to "control others without being controlled by others."

A specialized reading of the name of this school based on the same meanings for the characters *tsung* and *heng* can be best rendered by a colloquialism: *tsung-heng hsueh* means "the science of letting all hell break loose." This is a special sense of the term only in that it represents just one of the techniques of a more comprehensive learning.

Even in this sense, however, it can be construed in two ways. Where there is unrest that would only be exacerbated by direct confrontation, the unrest may be purposely allowed to burn itself out. Where there is complacency and lethargy, unrest may be deliberately triggered to produce reaction and movement.

Many of these techniques are well known through history, not only in China but all over the world. It is easy to see, just from the meanings of *tsung-heng hsueh*, and reflection on the obvious abuses to which these ideas are susceptible, why there has always been ambivalence and controversy surrounding this school of thought.

The contents of *The Master of Demon Valley* would lead us to suspect that *Tsung-heng hsueh* was either a splinter of Taoism or a separate school profoundly influenced by Taoism. A third possibility is that the Taoist element in the text, which is very prominent, represents a later attempt by philosophical Taoists to "encapsulate" the virulent ideas and practices of *Tsung-beng bsueh* in such a way as to mitigate harmful abuses.

In any case, the text of *The Master of Demon Valley* closes with this warning: "Petty people imitating others will use this in a perverse and sinister way, even getting to the point where they can destroy families and usurp countries. Without wisdom and knowledge, you cannot preserve your home with justice and cannot preserve your country with the Way. The reason sages value the subtlety of the Way is truly because it can change peril into safety, rescue the ruined and enable them to survive."

*The Master of the Hidden Storehouse* follows up on the implications of these statements regarding the science of power analyzed in *The Master of Demon Valley*. It is a classic Taoist text, following on the ancient philosophical tradition but adapted specifically for secular leaders.

*The Master of the Hidden Storehouse* is attributed to Keng Sang-tzu, who is featured in the Taoist classic *Chuang-tzu* as a disciple of the ancient sage Lao-tzu, traditionally considered the author of the *Tao Te Ching* and a seminal figure in Taoist lore.

Conventional scholars ordinarily consider *The Master of the Hidden Storehouse* an apocryphal text. While there is no actual proof of this assumption, based as it is on the supposition of a rigid division between oral and written traditions, there is every reason to believe, on the basis of classical principles, that the original core of the work was deliberately adapted to conditions of another time.

Nothing concrete is known of the text of *The Master of the Hidden Storehouse* until the T'ang dynasty, more than a thousand years after the time of the reputed author. This text was presented to the imperial court of T'ang China in the eighth century, in response to official efforts to reintegrate Taoist studies into the mainstream of intellectual life and scholastic curriculum. *The Master of the Hidden Storehouse* was so highly valued by the emperor Hsuan-tsung (r. 713–55) that it was given an honorific title, *Tung-ling ching* (*Dongling jing*), or "Scripture on Open Awareness."

*The Master of Demon Valley* and *The Master of the Hidden Storehouse* are both included in the vast canon of Taoism. The former text is unusually obscure, even for an ancient Taoist classic, indicating the antiquity of the oral tradition from which it derived as well as the concern of the early transmitters with safeguarding its knowledge from shallow meddlers. The latter text, in contrast, is unusually clear, even in distinguishing between exoteric and esoteric domains of learning, illustrating thereby its characteristic nature as a presentation of practical Taoism for general public purposes.

These two extraordinary texts complement, balance, and enhance one another; being therefore most profitably read together, in this their first rendition into English they are presented in one volume for the safety and convenience of the thoughtful reader.

# THE MASTER OF DEMON VALLEY

# OPENING AND CLOSING

## — 1 —

LET US CONSIDER HOW ancient sages existed between heaven and earth. Being leaders of others, they watched the opening and closing of yin and yang in order to direct people thereby and knew the doorway of survival and destruction. Assessing the ends and beginnings of all types, they arrived at the principles of human psychology and saw the foresigns of change therein; and they kept vigil at the doorway.

## — 2 —

Therefore the Way by which sages live in the world has always been one; while its transformations, which are endless, each has a specific purpose. Sometimes it is yin, sometimes yang; sometimes yielding, sometimes firm; sometimes open, sometimes closed; sometimes relaxed, sometimes tense. For this reason sages consistently keep watch at the doorway and carefully examine what should precede and what follow. They assess strategies, measure capabilities, and compare strengths and weaknesses of technical skills.

— 3 —

There are differences between the worthy and the unworthy, the intelligent and the foolish, the brave and the cowardly, the humane and the righteous; so it may be appropriate to open up, or to shut down; it may be appropriate to promote, or to demote; it may be appropriate to despise, or to value. Sages govern them without artificial contrivance. They carefully determine what people have and what they lack, in terms of their substantiality or vacuity. They follow what people like and desire, in order to observe their will and aspiration. They subtly brush aside what people say and press it back on them to find out what reality there is to it; and once they get the point, they clam up and put it into effect to find out what benefit there is to it.

— 4 —

Sages sometimes open up in an evident manner; sometimes they are closed and secretive. They are open to those with whom they sympathize, closed to those with whose truth they differ. As to what will do and what will not, sages examine and clarify people's plans to find out if they are in harmony or at variance.

— 5 —

Whether they separate or join, there is that which sages maintain; so they first go along with the aims of others: then when they want to open up, they value thoroughness; and when they want to shut down, they value secrecy. Thoroughness and secrecy are best subtle, for then they are on the trail of the Way.

— 6 —

Opening up is to assess people's feelings; shutting down is to make sure of their sincerity. In each case it is only after seeing people's plans and evaluating their worth that calculations are to be made for them; so sages make the relevant considerations on this basis. If people's plans do not measure up, and do not fit the dimensions and elements of the situation, then sages themselves therefore do the thinking. So opening up may be for the purpose of rejection, or for the purpose of acceptance; shutting down may be for the purpose of taking, or for the purpose of discarding.

— 7 —

Opening and closing are the Way of heaven and earth: opening and closing are used to transform and activate yin and yang and the four seasons; opening and closing are used to influence the rise and fall of all things. Maneuvers such as reversing to repel, reversing to cover up, and reversing to oppose, all have to come from this. Opening and closing are the great influences of the Way, changes of persuasion: it is necessary first to examine their transmutations.

— 8 —

The mouth is the door of the mind; the mind is the host of the spirit. Will, intention, joy, desire, thought, worry, knowledge, and planning all go in and out through the door. Therefore they are governed by opening and closing, controlled in their exit and entry. Opening means speech, or yang; closing means silence, or yin. Yin and yang should be harmonious; end and beginning should be correct.

— 9 —

Thus to talk of longevity, happiness, wealth, status, honor, fame, love, fondness, material gain, success, joy, or desire, is yang: this is called the beginning. And so to talk of death, grief, trouble, poverty, lowliness, disgrace, rejection, loss, disappointment, injury, punishment, execution, or penalty, is yin: this is called the end.

— 10 —

All speech in the yang category is called a beginning, meaning that one speaks of what is good in order to initiate projects. All speech in the yin category is called an ending, in that one speaks of what is bad in order to conclude strategic planning.

— 11 —

The course of opening and closing is proven by yin and yang. When speaking with those who are in a yang mode, go by the exalted and the lofty; when speaking with those who are in a yin mode, go by the humble and the small. Seek the small by lowliness, seek the great by loftiness. Follow this procedure, and what you say can be expressed anywhere, will penetrate anywhere, and can suit any situation. It will thereby be possible to persuade individuals, to persuade families, to persuade nations, to persuade the world.

## — 12 —

To be small means there is no inside; to be large means there is no outside. The phenomenal expressions of increase and reduction, rejection and acceptance, opposition and reversion, are all controlled by yin and yang. Yang is mobile and active; yin is still and unobtrusive. When yang emerges in activity, yin accordingly goes into concealment. When yang comes to an end, it returns to the beginning; and when yin reaches a climax, it reverts to yang.

## — 13 —

Using yang to act means development of character; using yin to be still means development of the body. Using yang to seek yin means enveloping with virtue; using yin to crystallize yang means exercise of power. The mutual seeking of yin and yang depends on opening and closing.

## — 14 —

This is the Way of yin and yang of heaven and earth; and it is the method of persuading people. Being the forerunner of all undertakings, it is called the door of the round and the square.

# RESPONSE

— 1 —

THE GREAT CIVILIZING INFLUENCE of ancient times arose together with the formless. By reflective examination of the past, you can investigate and check on the future; by reflective acquaintance with the ancient you can know the modern; by reflective understanding of others you can gain a clearer understanding of yourself. When principles of action and stillness, or emptiness and fullness, do not fit the present, then turn back to the past to look for them. The idea of the sages was that things have changes and can be reversed: it is imperative to examine closely.

— 2 —

The speech of others is movement; one's own silence is stillness. You listen to people's statements by means of their speech. When statements are inconsistent, reflect and inquire critically, and the response will surely be forthcoming.

— 3 —

Words have images, works have categories: observe their order by their images and categories. Images symbolize phenomena, categories group expressions. Use formlessness to inquire critically into that which is voiced. When statements made to draw people out are consistent with actualities, then you find out the reality in people.

— 4 —

When you set out snares to catch animals, you set many of them where the animals may be expected to run into them, and you watch over them. When your way is in conformity with actuality, others will emerge and come to you of their own accord: this is a net that catches people.

— 5 —

Always hold that net and motivate people. If there is nothing in your words to which they can relate, then you change for this reason. Use imagery to move them, in a manner responsive to their mentalities; seeing their feelings and states of mind, you can govern them accordingly. If you yourself turn around and go to them, they will turn around and come to you. When speech contains images and analogies, by their means you can establish a foundation. Repeat them over and over, reflect on them over and over, and the appropriate rhetoric and expressions for all affairs will not be lost.

## — 6 —

Those whom sages attract do not doubt, be they ignorant or intelligent. Therefore those who are skilled at reflective listening change ghosts and spirits so as to be able to find out their feelings. When the change is appropriate, they are governed knowledgeably. If they are not governed knowledgeably, their feelings are not clearly apprehended; and if their feelings are not clearly apprehended, then the establishment of the foundation is not done with clear understanding.

## — 7 —

When you change images and analogies, there are bound to be words of opposition; listen to them in silence. When you want to hear others' voices, return to silence; when you want to be expansive, then be withdrawn; when you want to rise, then lower yourself; when you want to take, then give.

## — 8 —

When you want to bring out feelings and states of mind, use symbolism and analogies to muster the appropriate expressions: those with the same voice call to each other, true principles have the same ultimate end. Sometimes the process starts from you, sometimes from another; sometimes it is used to work for superiors, sometimes it is used to govern subordinates.

—9—

This is listening for reality and artifice, to know whether there is commonality or difference, and to find out truth and falsehood. In any case, it is by first making these determinations that it is possible to formulate appropriate guidelines. This procedure is used because you seek to convert others by questioning them and observing what their feelings depend upon.

— 10 —

You need to be equanimous and calm yourself in order to listen to people's statements, examine their affairs, assess myriad things, and distinguish relative merits. Even if you repudiate specific matters, see their subtleties and know their types. If you are searching into people and live in their midst, you can measure their abilities and see into their intentions, with never a failure to tally.

— 11 —

Therefore, knowledge begins from knowing yourself; after that you can know others. This interrelated knowledge is likened to a mythological fish that has only one eye and thus must travel in pairs. With this knowledge, perception of form is like the relationship of light and shadow; then you can see into words without missing anything, like a magnet attracting needles. Your dealings with people are subtle, your perception of their feelings and mental states is quick. It is like yin to yang, like yang to yin; it is like round to square, like square to round.

## — 12 —

Before you can see formations, you guide people in a rounded way; once formations have taken shape, you employ people with rectitude. In matters of promotion and demotion, dismissal or honor, you use this method to oversee them. If you have not made the appropriate determinations yourself beforehand, the way you govern people will not be correct.

## — 13 —

When affairs are handled unskillfully, this is called ignorance of feelings and loss of the Way. When you have thoroughly clarified matters yourself, and have determined measures whereby it is possible to govern others, and yet you reveal no obvious form, so that no one can see into your privacy, this is called genius.

# ACCEPTANCE AND SOLIDARITY

— 1 —

IN THE RELATIONSHIP BETWEEN ruler and minister, or between superior or subordinate, there may be those who are on friendly terms in spite of distance, and there may be those who are alienated in spite of closeness.

— 2 —

Someone who tries to cleave to a ruler may not be employed, while someone who leaves a ruler may on the contrary be sought after.

— 3 —

There may be those who come forward day after day but are not taken seriously, and there may be those who are heard of from afar yet are given consideration.

— 4 —

In all affairs there has to be acceptance and solidarity to form the basic bonding at the start. Ties may be made by virtue, by partisanship, by money, or by sex.

## — 5 —

When you go by others' wishes, then get involved when they want to get involved, stay away when they want to stay away, approach when they want to approach, be distant when they want to be distant, join up when they want to join up, depart when they want to depart, seek when they want to seek, think when they want to think.

## — 6 —

This is like a mother ground-spider following the needs of her offspring: when she leaves her burrow, she leaves no gap; and when she goes back into her burrow, she leaves no trace. She goes out independently and comes back independently, and no one can stop her.

## — 7 —

Acceptance is a matter of presenting convincing statements; solidarity is a matter of holding firmly to what is planned. Those who wish to be convincing strive to make their calculations in secret; those who plan things strive to follow orderly procedures.

## — 8 —

By inwardly considering what is appropriate and what is not, then clearly stating what is advantageous and what is harmful, it is possible to direct another's will.

— 9 —

When measures are brought forth in response to the time, thus do they accord with appropriate strategy. Think over carefully what to bring up, and when you go forth you respond to the necessities of the time.

— 10 —

Now, if there is disharmony within them, measures cannot be carried out. Then figure out what is appropriate for the time, and change what you do accordingly, in order to seek a suitable adaptation.

— 11 —

Seeking acceptance by adaptation is like a lock taking a key. When speaking of the past, first use conventional terms; when speaking of the future, use adaptable words.

— 12 —

Those who are expert at adaptation examine the lay of the land and understand nature; thereby they transform the four seasons and make ghosts and spirits harmonize with yin and yang. Thus do they govern people: seeing the things they plan, they know their aspirations and intentions.

## — 13 —

When there is disharmony in affairs, that means there is something unknown. When there is collusion but not solidarity, there is overt alliance but covert alienation. When there is disharmony in affairs, sages do not make plans for them.

## — 14 —

Thus when there is intimacy in spite of distance, that means there is hidden virtue. When there is alienation in spite of nearness, that means there is disparity of aims.

## — 15 —

Those who try to cleave to rulers but are not employed are those whose plans are ineffective; those who leave rulers but then are sought after are those who are subsequently proven to be right.

## — 16 —

Those who come forward day after day but are not taken seriously are those whose proposals are inappropriate; those who are heard of from afar yet are given consideration are those who fit in with plans and are counted on to decide matters.

— 17 —

Therefore it is said that those who speak without seeing what type of person they are talking to will be opposed, and those who speak without finding out the state of mind of the person they are talking to will be denied.

— 18 —

When you apprehend people's feelings and states of mind, then you can use your arts masterfully. Applying this method you can put people off, and can bring them in; you can form ties with people, and can separate yourself from them.

— 19 —

Therefore when sages set things up, they use this means to get to know people beforehand and establish solidarity with them. Based on reason, virtue, humanity, justice, courtesy, and culture, they figure out plans.

— 20 —

First they take up classical poetry and documents, mixing in talk of loss and gain, considering what to abandon and what to take up. Those with whom they wish to collaborate, they deliberately admit; those of whom they want to be rid, they deliberately exclude.

## —21—

In order to exclude or admit effectively, it is necessary to understand the logic of the Way, figure out coming events, and settle any doubts that are sensed. Then there will be no miscalculation in the measures taken, which will then be successful and worthwhile.

## —22—

To direct a populace in productive work is called solidarity and inner cooperation. If the leadership is ignorant and cannot manage, those below get confused without even realizing it; reverse this by solidarity. If the leadership is self-satisfied and pays no attention to what outsiders have to say, then laud it to the skies. If a summons comes spontaneously, then rise to it and take over command. If you want to leave, then give up on account of danger.

## —23—

Adapt fluidly to changes, and no one will know what you are doing; you accomplish great things while remaining in the background.

# STOPPING GAPS

## — 1 —

THINGS HAVE NATURAL COURSES; events have combinations and divisions. There is that which is near but cannot be seen; there is that which is remote and yet can be known. The near at hand is unseen when you do not examine what is said; the remote can be known when you question the past to discern the future.

## — 2 —

A gap is an opening; an opening is a space between barriers; a space between barriers makes for tremendous vulnerability. At the first sign of a gap, it should be shored up, or repelled, or stopped, or hidden, or overwhelmed. These are called the principles of stopping gaps.

## — 3 —

When things are perilous, sages know it, and preserve themselves in solitude. They explain things according to developments, and thoroughly master strategy, whereby they discern the subtle. Starting from the slightest beginnings, they work against tremendous odds. What they provide to the outside world, strategies for nipping problems in the bud, all depend on stopping gaps. Stopping gaps is an application of the arts of the Way.

— 4 —

When the land is in confusion, there is no enlightened leadership above, and the public officials have no real virtue. Then petty people slander and despoil, wise people are not employed, and sages go into hiding. Greedy connivers go into action, rulers and ministers confuse each other, fall out with each other and attack each other. Parents and children separate, and there is rebellion and antagonism. These are called budding gaps.

— 5 —

When sages see budding gaps, they plug them up with laws. If society can thereby be ordered, then they stop up the gaps. If it is unruly, they overwhelm them. Sometimes they attack the problem in one way, sometimes another: sometimes they attack in such a way as to effect a restoration, sometimes they attack in such a way as to effect an overthrow.

— 6 —

Ever since there has been the cyclic process of combination and separation of heaven and earth, there have always been gaps. It is imperative to see into them. The purpose of seeing into them is to be able to open and close them. One who can apply this principle is a sage.

## —7—

Sages are servants of heaven and earth: if society is in an irremediable state, they hide deeply and await the right time to act. In a time when something can be done, they plan for it. They can accord with the higher, they can regulate the lower; able to follow, able to conform, they are guardian spirits of heaven and earth.

# Excitation and arrest

## — 1 —

In general, assessing strategy and measuring ability is instrumental in attracting those far away and drawing them near.

## — 2 —

To establish power and control affairs, first it is imperative to discern sameness and difference: to distinguish right and wrong speech, see expressions of what is inside and what is outside, know the logic of what is and what is not, decide which plans are safe and which dangerous, and determine what is nearby and what is far off.

## — 3 —

After that you can weigh and measure: and if there are ways to correct errors, then you can call for them, find them, and employ them.

## — 4 —

By using "hooking and clamping" expressions, you can excite and arrest people. Hooking and clamping talk involves speaking in a manner that is now the same, now different. Considering the thoughts going on in their minds, examine their ideas to know what they like and dislike; then speak of what they value, using exciting and arresting words to hold them fast by hooking onto what they like.

—5—

As for those who cannot be managed well, you may first invite them, then lay a heavy responsibility on them. Or you may first belabor them with a heavy responsibility, and then criticize them afterward. Or you may use a heavy responsibility itself to tear them down, or tear them down in order to lay a heavy responsibility on them.

—6—

If you are going to employ people, you may assess their attitudes toward money, material goods, and sex, in order to position them accordingly. Or you may assess their abilities, empower them, and thereby hook them. Or you may watch them, and clamp down when you see an opening. These practices depend on stopping gaps.

—7—

When you are going to use this on a whole land, it is imperative to assess power and measure abilities, to perceive the waxing and waning of natural timing, to control the lay of the land, to know the difficult and easy terrain, to determine how much or little money and goods the people have, and to know which of the local leaders with whom you associate are friendly and which are distant, which of them like you and which of them dislike you.

— 8 —

Once you have examined people's mentalities, intentions, and thoughts, and gotten to know what they like and dislike, then you speak of what is important to them, using intoxicating and arresting expressions to hook into their inclinations and thereby hold them and attract them.

— 9 —

When you use this on individual people, you measure their knowledge and ability, weigh their talents and strengths, calculate their energy and force, and then devise means of regulating and controlling them. You may go out to meet them, then go along with them to bond and harmonize, using their own ideas to get through to them. This is the linkage of intoxication and arrest.

— 10 —

When you use this on people, it starts out unreal but comes to be real. Link up unerringly, thus finding out the truth or

otherwise of what they say, and you can control their obedience and control their freedom: you can lead them in any
direction, and can lead them to reverse themselves, or even
overturn. And even if they are overturned, you can restore
them, without losing appropriate measure.

# OPPOSITION AND ALLIANCE

## — 1 —

IN MATTERS OF RAPPROCHEMENT, alliance, rejection, and revolution, there are suitable strategies. Adapting to changes fluidly, each has a configuration, regulated according to events.

## — 2 —

Therefore sages dwell between heaven and earth, cultivate themselves, govern society, dispense education, elevate the reputable, and clarify terms. In doing so, they always use the opportunities afforded by events and phenomena, observing the timing of Nature. Based on this, they know what to increase and what to decrease. By knowing all this beforehand, they can adapt to changes.

## — 3 —

The world has no fixed values, events have no fixed guide. Sages have no fixed involvements, yet there is nothing they do not affect. They listen to nothing, yet there is nothing they do not hear. If they are successful in what they do and appropriate in their planning, they are made into leaders.

— 4 —

If plans are suitable for one party but not for another, then they are not faithful to both sides. There must be contrast and opposition. To return to one side, you oppose the other; to oppose one side, you return to the other. This is the technique.

— 5 —

When you use this technique on a nation, you must evaluate the nation before applying it. When you use it on a state, you must evaluate the state before applying it. When you use it on a household, you must evaluate the household before applying it. When you use it on an individual, you must evaluate the individual's capacity and power before applying it. Whether on a large or small scale, advancing or withdrawing, the function is the same. It is imperative to first think strategically and determine a plan before putting it into action by means of the art of intoxication and arrest.

— 6 —

In ancient times, those who were skilled in using rejection and acceptance brought about cooperation within the four seas, enveloping the grounds of local leaders' disputes and alliances, and transforming them, after that seeking unity thereby.

## —7—

That is why Yi Yin went to King T'ang five times and King Chieh five times without being able to clarify anything; only later did he join with T'ang. Lu Shang went to King Wen three times, entering the palace three times, without being able to clarify anything; only later did he join with King Wen. They knew the clamp of the decree of Heaven, so they accepted it without doubt.

## —8—

Only perfect sages of profound understanding can direct society. Without mental effort and intense thought, one cannot get to the bottom of things. Without understanding mentalities and perceiving feelings, one cannot attain success. One with talent but no kindness cannot command an army. One with loyalty but no reality cannot know people.

## —9—

Therefore the method of opposition and alliance demands that you gauge your own ability and intelligence, and assess your own strengths and weaknesses, seeing who does not compare among those far and near. Only then can you advance and withdraw freely and independently.

# FIGURING OUT
# PSYCHOLOGICAL CONDITIONS

## — 1 —

THOSE IN ANCIENT TIMES who skillfully operated countries always measured the powers in the land and figured out the psychological conditions of local leaders. If measurement of powers is not thorough, you do not know the strong and the weak, the light and the heavy. If psychological conditions are not figured out thoroughly, you do not know the activities of hidden changes and developments.

## — 2 —

What does it mean to measure powers? It means to calculate the size of territory, how many or few participate in planning, how much there is in the way of money and goods, how big the population is, how rich or poor the people are, whether they have surpluses or shortages, where the terrain is dangerous and where it is easy, what is advantageous and what is harmful, whose strategy is better, whether the leadership and the administrators are close or distant, who is worthy and who is unworthy, and whose hired counselors are more intelligent.

— 3 —

Observe whether the seasons bode ill or well, and see whether the alliances of local leaders are useful or not. Observe the minds of the common people, how they behave and how they change, whether they are secure or insecure, who they like and who they hate, and who is in a position to rebel. If you can ascertain all of this, that is called measuring powers.

— 4 —

As for figuring out psychological conditions, you must go to people when they are in a very good mood, and emphasize what they want; then if they have desires, they will not be able to hide their feelings. And you must go to people when they are in a very fearful mood, and emphasize what they dislike; then if they have aversions, they will not be able to hide their feelings. Feelings and desires inevitably emerge when people go through changes.

— 5 —

When they are emotionally stirred but you still do not discern how they change, then leave such people alone and do not talk to them. Instead, question their familiars to find out where their feelings and desires lie.

— 6 —

When psychological conditions change within, physical manifestations appear outwardly. Therefore it is always necessary to discern what is concealed by way of what is visible. This is what is called fathoming the depths and figuring out psychological conditions.

— 7 —

Therefore, those who would plan national affairs should carefully examine the quantity of power; those who would persuade leaders should carefully figure out psychological conditions. Strategic consideration of psychological conditions and desires must emerge from this. Then it is possible to ennoble and to demean, to esteem and to belittle, to help and to harm, to bring about success and to bring about failure: the formula is one and the same.

— 8 —

Therefore, even if you have the Way of ancient kings and the strategy of sages, unless you figure out psychological conditions there is no way for you to find out what is hidden. This is the basis of strategy, and also the method of persuasion. You are always one up on other people, and none can precede you. To get there before events arise is most difficult to do.

## — 9 —

So it is said that figuring out psychological conditions is most difficult to master. This means that it is necessary to time strategic thinking appropriately.

## — 10 —

Thus if you observe how everyone and everything, even down to insects, can be beneficial in some way and harmful in some way, then you can produce excellence in undertakings. What gives rise to undertakings is subtle momentum. This is to be discussed after having figured out psychological conditions and framed them in elegant expression.

# PRESSURING

## — 1 —

PRESSURING IS A TECHNIQUE for figuring people out. Inner correspondence is the subject figured out. There is a Way to employ this; that Way is necessarily covert and subtle.

## — 2 —

Pressure people with what they desire in order to sound them out, and the inner correspondence will inevitably respond. What they respond to is what they would surely do.

## — 3 —

Therefore you subtly stand apart from this. That is called shutting off openings, hiding the point, concealing what you like to avoid emotions, so that no one knows what you are doing, and therefore you can accomplish your task without trouble.

## — 4 —

Pressuring is up to you; response is up to others. When you use this accordingly, nothing is impossible.

— 5 —

Those in ancient times who were skilled at pressuring were as if fishing in a deep body of water, casting in bait and never failing to catch fish therein. In this sense it is said that when you direct affairs you succeed day after day, yet nobody knows; when you direct the military you win day after day, yet nobody fears.

— 6 —

Sages plan this in secret, so they are called genius; they carry it out in the open, so they are called enlightened.

— 7 —

Daily success in directing affairs means accumulating virtue, so that the people feel secure yet are not conscious of why they have benefited; it means accumulating goodness, so that the people are guided by it without knowing why it is so. Thus everyone compares this to genius and enlightenment.

— 8 —

Daily victory in directing the military means battling not to fight, not to waste, so the people do not know why they submit and do not know of a reason to fear. So everyone compares this to genius and enlightenment.

—9—

The pressuring may be done by means of placidity, or by means of correctness, or by means of joy, or by means of anger, or by means of reputation, or by means of action, or by means of honesty, or by means of faith, or by means of profit, or by means of abasement.

— 10 —

Placidity means silence. Correctness means appropriateness. Joy means pleasing. Anger means stirring. Reputation means motivating. Action means accomplishing. Honesty means moral purity. Faith means expectation. Profit means seeking. Abasement means flattery.

— 11 —

Thus the reason that sages alone employ all this is that while it is available to everyone, yet no one does it successfully, because they use it wrongly.

— 12 —

So in pressuring there is nothing more difficult than thoroughness. In persuasion there is nothing more difficult than being heard completely. In doing things there is nothing more difficult than ensuring success. These three can be handled only by sages.

## — 13 —

Therefore strategy must arise from thoroughness. It is imperative to choose something in common as a medium of persuasion. This is why it is said that there may be bonding that has no gaps.

## — 14 —

When undertakings succeed, they invariably conform to logic. Therefore it is said that the logic of the Way is partner to the time.

## — 15 —

When persuasion is accepted, it invariably conforms to feelings. Therefore it is said that when feelings meet there is acceptance; people listen to those with compatible feelings.

## — 16 —

So beings return to kind. Of those who run to a bonfire with an armload of kindling, the fastest burn first. When water is poured on level ground, a moist patch will absorb it first. This is natural correspondence between things of a kind; power configurations and momenta are also like this. This means that inner correspondence responding to external pressure is like this.

Therefore it is said, "Pressure people according to their affinities; if there is no response, then pressure them by what they desire." There are those who do not listen or accept, so it is called a path that is traveled alone. Those who perceive the subtle and see opportunities are not late; they succeed without getting caught up in it, and eventually their civilizing influence fully develops.

# ASSESSMENT

## —1—

PERSUASION IS A MATTER of convincing or pleasing others. When you persuade people, you take your material from them. When you embellish words, you are borrowing them; when you borrow them you adjust them.

## —2—

Answering responsively is a matter of convenient expression; convenient expression is light discourse. Being meaningful means clarifying; clarification is a matter of tallying with experience.

## —3—

Talk may go back and forth, indicating an inclination to mutual rejection. Critical words are opposing argument. Opposing argument fishes out subtleties.

## —4—

Crafty talk uses flattery in seeking to appear loyal. Ingratiating talk uses breadth in seeking to appear knowledgeable. Grandiose talk uses determination in seeking to appear brave. Concerned talk uses calculation in seeking to appear trustworthy. Calm talk uses opposition in seeking to appear victorious.

— 5 —

Anticipating wishes and catering to desires is flattery. Abundant quotation of literature is breadth. Abandon without hesitation is determination. Planning, making choices, and developing tactics is calculating. Discerning insufficiency to stop error is opposition.

— 6 —

Therefore the mouth is a mechanism, by means of which one can shut up feelings and ideas. Ears and eyes are assistants of the mind, means of seeing through treachery and perversion. Therefore it is said that when these three respond in harmony, they act in a beneficial way.

— 7 —

So those who say a lot without confusion, who soar to the heights and go back and forth and all around without getting lost, who change without being imperiled, have seen the essential principle.

## — 8 —

Colors and forms cannot be shown to the blind, voices and music cannot be conveyed to the deaf. So those to whom you should not go are those whom you have no means of enlightening, and those who cannot come to you are those to whom you are not receptive. Some people do not understand, so sages do not work for them.

## — 9 —

An ancient said, "The mouth should be used for eating rather than speaking," because there are taboos about what can be said; "the mouths of the masses can melt metal," because words have nuances that can be twisted.

## — 10 —

Human feelings are such that when people speak, they want to be heard; and when they undertake things, they want to succeed. Therefore wise people do not use the weaknesses of the ignorant but their strengths; they do not use the clumsiness of the ignorant, but use their skills: they are not frustrated. That means they follow the strengths of those who can be of help, and avoid the weaknesses of those who can do harm.

## — 11 —

So the defense of insects with shells necessitates thickness and hardness in the shell; the action of poisonous insects necessitates a venomous sting. Thus birds and beasts know how to employ their strengths, while speakers know what is useful and use it.

## — 12 —

So it is said that there are five kinds of verbal expression, conveying affliction, fear, anxiety, anger, and joy. Affliction involves a sense of declining energy and a lack of liveliness. Fear involves such extreme upset that there is no self-control. Anxiety is suffocating, with no outlet. Anger involves arbitrary stirring and unruliness. Joy involves being scattered and lacking concentration. These five you can use if you are an expert; if they are beneficial, then put them into action.

## — 13 —

Thus when talking with the knowledgeable, base it on breadth; when talking with the broadly learned, base it on discernment; when talking with the discerning, base it on quintessential focus. When talking with those of high status, base it on power; when talking with the wealthy, base it on loftiness. When talking with the poor, base it on profit; when talking with the lowly, base it on modesty. When talking with the courageous, base it on bravery; when talking with the ignorant, base it on acuity.

— 14 —

This is the art; but people usually do the opposite. For this reason, when speaking to people with knowledge, you use this to enlighten them; when speaking to people without knowledge, you use this to educate them, but it is very hard to do.

— 15 —

So, talk is of many kinds, affairs undergo many changes. Thus if your talk is always of the appropriate kind, your affairs will not be disorderly; if you never change, you do not lose your autonomy.

— 16 —

Thus when it comes to knowledge, what is important is not to forget; when it comes to listening, what is important is to be clear; when it comes to wisdom, what is important is to understand; and when it comes to rhetoric, what is important is to be exceptional.

# STRATEGIC THINKING

## — 1 —

ALL STRATEGY HAS A WAY, which demands that you find the bases to discover the conditions. Having carefully examined and apprehended conditions, then you set up three categories: higher, middling, and lower. These three having been established, you use them to produce unexpected strategies, which will not know any obstacle. This begins with following the perennial.

## — 2 —

Thus people on a treasure hunt use a compass to avoid getting lost: measuring capacities, assessing abilities, and figuring out feelings and psychological conditions are the compass of business and political affairs.

## — 3 —

So when two parties who share the same feelings are on friendly terms, that means they are both succeeding; when two parties have the same wishes and yet are estranged, that means one side is getting hurt. When those with the same aversions are friendly, that means they are both getting hurt; when those with the same aversions are estranged, that means only one party is getting hurt.

— 4 —

Thus when people profit each other they are friendly, and when they cause each other loss they become estranged; it is the operation of natural law. This is a means of perceiving the separation between difference and sameness.

— 5 —

So a wall crumbles at the seams, wood breaks at a knot: this is the significance of separation.

— 6 —

Thus changes give rise to tasks, tasks give rise to strategy, strategy gives rise to planning, planning gives rise to discussion, discussion gives rise to persuasion, persuasion gives rise to progress, progress gives rise to withdrawal, withdrawal gives rise to control. By thus controlling affairs, everything can be accomplished in the same way, following the same principles every time.

— 7 —

Now then, humane people think lightly of wealth, so they cannot be seduced by profit, but they can be induced to make expenditures. Brave people think lightly of difficulty, so they cannot be intimidated by trouble, but they can be gotten to manage perilous situations. Wise people are perfectly logical and reasonable, so they cannot be fooled by untruth, but they can be edified by truth and induced to perform worthy deeds. These are three types of ability.

— 8 —

Thus it is easy to blind the ignorant, easy to intimidate the unworthy, and easy to seduce the avaricious. This is a matter of dealing with them according to actualities.

— 9 —

Therefore those who are strong have built it up from weakness; those who are straightforward have built it up from tact; and those who have a surplus have built it up from lack. This is the action of the relevant arts of the Way.

— 10 —

So if there is outward friendliness but inward estrangement, reconcile the inner relationship. If there is inward friendliness but outward estrangement, reconcile the outward relationship. Thus you change others based on their doubts, affirm them based on their views, make pacts with them based on what they say, reinforce them based on what they do, assess them based on what they dislike, fend them off by what distresses them. Frighten them by pressure, stir them by excitement, prove them by surrounding, confuse them by disturbance—these are called tactical strategies.

## — 11 —

In the use of tactical strategies, it is better to be private than public; and alliance is even better than mere privacy, alliance meaning a partnership that has no gaps. It is better to be unconventional than conventional, the unconventional being that which flows unceasingly. So when persuading leaders, it is imperative to talk to them of the unconventional; when persuading administrators, it is imperative to talk to them privately.

## — 12 —

Those who are themselves on the inside but speak to outsiders are ostracized. Those who are themselves outsiders but whose talk goes too deep are in danger. What people do not like should not be forced on them; what does not concern people should not be taught to them.

## — 13 —

When people have likes, learn them and adapt to them. When people have dislikes, avoid them and do not mention them. Thus you make your way covertly, yet gain the result openly. Therefore when you are going to get rid of people, you indulge them, then get rid of those who do indulge.

## — 14 —

When people's appearances are neither too attractive nor too repulsive, they are wholeheartedly trusted. Those who can be known can be employed; those who are inscrutable are not employed by planners.

## — 15 —

So it is said that in professional affairs it is considered important to control others, not to be controlled by others. Controlling people means holding power and authority; being controlled by people means your life and fate are controlled. Therefore the Way of sages is covert, while the way of the ignorant is obvious.

## — 16 —

It is easy to work for the wise, hard to work for the unwise. From this perspective, since what makes for destruction cannot produce survival, and what makes for danger cannot produce safety, there is nothing to do but value wisdom.

## — 17—

Wisdom employs what is unknown to most people, and can use what is invisible to most people. Once wisdom is in use, seeing what can be chosen and doing it is how one acts on one's own; seeing that which affords no choice and doing it is how one acts for others.

## — 18 —

Therefore the Way of ancient kings is unseen. A saying has it, "The evolution of heaven and earth is in the heights and the depths; the sages' Way of mastery is in concealment and covertness. It is not just faithfulness, truthfulness, humanity, and justice; it is a matter of balance and accuracy."

## — 19 —

When people's reasoning has arrived at the meaning of this, then they are worth talking to. Through attainment of this, it is possible to bring in the just from far and near.

# DECISION MAKING

N

## — 1 —

ALL DECISION MAKING IS based on doubt. What enables people to prosper they consider good; what involves trouble they consider bad. The consummation of skill in this matter is to draw others; if there is ultimately no confusion or bias, then there is benefit in it. Eliminate the benefit, and a decision is not accepted. This is the reason for unorthodox tactics.

## — 2 —

When there is benefit for good, but it is concealed and made out to be bad, then a decision is not accepted, and produces alienation. Thus it is possible to cause loss of benefit, or even cause harm; these are slips in business and political affairs.

## — 3 —

The means by which sages can accomplish their tasks are five. They may do it by overt benevolence, or they may do it by covert attack. They may do it by use of honesty, or they may do it by cover-up. They may also use plain simplicity.

— 4 —

Yang is diligent at one word, Yin is diligent at two words: [1] simplicity; and [2] essential function. Using four things, exercise them subtly. Now assess past events as an indication of future events, compare this with the ordinary, and if appropriate you decide on that.

— 5 —

In the affairs of rulers, the general public, or important people, if something lofty and noble is possible and appropriate, decision is made in favor of that. If something that does not require expenditure of energy and is easy to accomplish is possible and appropriate, decision is made in favor of that. If something that requires effort and intense exertion but cannot be avoided is possible and appropriate, decision is made in favor of that. Decision is made in favor of that which eliminates trouble, if possible and appropriate; decision is made in favor of that which leads to good fortune, if possible and appropriate.

— 6 —

So determining conditions and settling doubts are the foundations of all tasks. To bring order to chaos correctly and determine success and failure are difficult to do. That is why ancient kings even used oracles to decide for themselves.

# TALISMANIC SAYINGS

## — 1 —

BE PEACEFUL, EASYGOING, UPRIGHT, and calm; then the measures you impose will be accommodating. If you are good at managing but are not calm, then empty your heart and even your mind, and wait for unease to fall away. This helps master rank.

## — 2 —

Eyes and ears should be clear; the mind should be wise. Those who see through everyone's eyes see everything; those who hear through everyone's ears hear everything; those who think through everyone's minds know everything. When all of these are combined and advanced together, then understanding cannot be blocked. This helps master understanding.

## — 3 —

The art of virtue is this: do not be stiff and forbidding. When you are forgiving, then you are protected; when you are forbidding, then you are shut off. Even a high mountain can be seen all the way to the top, and even a deep body of water can be measured; but the upright calm of the art of virtue practiced by the spiritually enlightened is unfathomable. This helps master virtue.

— 4 —

A system of rewards should be reliable; a system of punishments should be correct. That the giving of rewards should be reliable means that it is imperative to prove what eyes and ears see and hear. As for those who are not heard of or noticed, none will fail to be unconsciously influenced. Truthfulness is expressed for the world and the spirits, so the treacherous can hardly affect the leader. This helps master reward.

— 5 —

First consider heaven, second earth, third humanity. In the four directions, the zenith and the nadir, left and right, in front and behind: where does ill omen lie? This helps master inquiry.

— 6 —

The mind is the government of nine openings, the ruler is the chief of five officials. To those who do good, the ruler gives rewards; to those who do wrong, the ruler metes out penalties. When the ruler gives according to what is sought, then there is no toil or trouble. Sages apply this, and therefore are competent at giving rewards. Following reason based on this, then they are able to last a long time. This helps master logic.

— 7 —

Leaders should not fail to be comprehensive. If leaders are not comprehensive, the multitudes of administrators will create confusion and business will be erratic. When those on the inside and those on the outside do not communicate, how do they know what to express? When expressiveness and reticence are not skillful, you do not see the source. This helps master comprehensiveness.

— 8 —

First, extend your vision; second, widen your information; third, stabilize your clarity of mind. When you clearly know what is going on covertly a thousand miles away, this is called spying out all the villains in the world, so none are not unknowingly changed. This helps master respect.

— 9 —

When actualities do in fact accord with names, there is peace and wholeness. Names and actualities give rise to each other; they turn into conditions of one another. Therefore it is said, "When names are accurate, they give rise to actualities; actualities give rise to principles; principles produce the virtues of names and actualities; virtues produce harmony; harmony gives rise to accuracy." This helps master naming.

# BASIC COURSE: SEVEN ARTS OF COVERT CORRESPONDENCE

✎

*A. Invigorating the spirit: the method is modeled
on the five dragons.*

— 1 —

WITHIN THE INVIGORATED SPIRIT are five energies. The spirit
is their leader, the mind is their abode, virtue is their chief.
The place to develop energy is ultimately the Way.

— 2 —

The Way is the origin of heaven and earth; the One is their
foundation. Whatever is made by things or produced by nature contains a formless developmental energy, which was
there before heaven and earth: no one can see its form, and
no one knows its name; it is called spiritual and miraculous.

— 3 —

So the Way is the source of spiritual illumination: unity is
the beginning of its evolution. Through this virtue one nur-

tures the five energies: if the mind can be unified, you will attain the art.

$$-4-$$

The art is that whereby the Way of mental energy is housed; the spirit acts as its functionary. The senses are the gateways of energy, under the general control of the mind.

$$-5-$$

Our life as received from Nature is called real human being. Real human beings are one with Nature. Those who inwardly cultivate refinement with this knowledge are called sages.

$$-6-$$

Sages know things by analogy. People are born with oneness, then develop changes along with things. Discerning types is up to the senses; if there is any doubt or confusion, it is penetrated by mental technique. If the mind lacks appropriate technique, there will inevitably be failure to penetrate. With this penetration, the five energies are nurtured. The task is a matter of sheltering the spirit. This is called development.

$$-7-$$

Development involves five energies, including will, thought, spirit, and character. Spirit is the unifying leader. Calmness and harmony nurture energy; when energy attains the right harmony, then will, thought, spirit, and character do not deteriorate, and these four facets of force and power all thereby survive and stay there. This is called spiritual development ending up in the body; this is what we call the real human being.

— 8 —

Real humans assimilate to Nature and merge with the Way: holding to unity, they nurture and produce myriad things. Embracing the heart of Nature, they disburse blessings and nourishment; while enveloping all with noncontrivance, they act on power only with deliberate reflection and thoughtful intention. When people can master this invigoration of spirit, then they can develop will.

### B. Developing the will: the method is modeled on the spirit-tortoise.

— 1 —

Development of will is for when the energy of mind does not reach the intended object. When you have some desire, your will dwells on it and intends it. Will is a functionary of desire. When you have many desires, then your mind is scattered; when your mind is scattered, then your will deteriorates. When your will deteriorates, then thought does not attain its object.

## — 2 —

Therefore, if the energy of the mind is unified then desires do not roam around. When desires do not roam around then will does not deteriorate. When will does not deteriorate, then thought of true reason reaches its object.

## — 3 —

When true reason is reached, then harmony pervades. When harmony pervades, then unruly energy does not trouble the heart. So inwardly you thereby develop will, while outwardly you thereby get to know people. When you develop will, then your mind is penetrating and perceptive; when you know people, then the division of labor is clear.

## — 4 —

If you are going to use this in dealing with people, it is imperative first to know their development of energy and will. Knowing how robust or deteriorated people's energy is, you nurture their willpower and examine what makes them feel secure in order to know what they are capable of doing.

— 5 —

If will is not developed, then the energy of mind is not stable. If the energy of mind is not stable, then thought and reflection do not arrive at understanding. When thought and reflection do not arrive at understanding, then intent and will are insubstantial. When intent and will are insubstantial, then response is not powerful. When response is not powerful, then will is lost and the heart is drained. When the heart is drained, then the spirit is lost. When the spirit is lost, that results in vagueness; with vagueness, the combination of mind, spirit, and will is not unified.

— 6 —

In the beginning of developing will, the thing to do is to make yourself peaceful. Making yourself peaceful is a matter of substantiality and stability of will. When the will is substantial and stable, then your power is not fragmented. When spiritual illumination always keeps you secure, then you can impart this.

### C. Solidifying intent: the method is modeled on a supernatural serpent.

— 1 —

Solidifying intent refers to the formulation of mental energy into thought. The mind should be calm and quiet, thought should be deep and far-reaching. When the mind is calm and quiet, then brilliant measures are conceived; when thought is deep and far-reaching, then strategic plans are perfected. When brilliant measures are conceived, then the will cannot be disturbed. When strategic plans are perfected, then achievements cannot be blocked.

— 2 —

When intent and thought are stabilized, then the mind is easygoing and peaceful. When the mind is easygoing and peaceful, then its activities are not mistaken, and the spirit is self-possessed, and being self-possessed is therefore stable.

— 3 —

Perceptibly manifest energies or moods are acquired; treachery can subdue them and fraud can confuse them, so that what is said does not come from the heart. Therefore the mental art of the trustworthy is to maintain true unity unchanging, awaiting the interaction of people's ideas and thoughts, listening to them and watching them.

— 4 —

Strategic planning is the pivot of survival and destruction: if thinking is not fitting, then hearing is not clear, and timing is inaccurate, resulting in mistakes in planning. Then intention is unreliable; it is vacuous and insubstantial. Therefore in strategic thinking, the thing to do is solidify intent; and solidification of intent must begin with mental technique.

— 5 —

Seeking by noncontrivance calms and tunes the internal organs: when the vitality, spirit, celestial soul, and earthly soul are steadfastly kept unmoving, then you can look inward and listen backward, settling will and thought in the cosmic void, helping the going and coming of the spirit.

— 6 —

Thereby you observe the opening and closing of heaven and earth, discern the creations of myriad things, and see the governance of human affairs. You know the whole world without going out the door, you see the course of heaven without looking through the window, you direct without seeing, arrive without going: this is called the knowledge of the Way, whereby you become attuned to spiritual illumination, respond to the unexpected, and are imbued with spirit.

### D. Dividing power: the method is modeled on a crouching bear.

— 1 —

Dividing power is a matter of being enveloped in the spirit: so quiet your mind and stabilize your will so that the spirit returns to its abode; then you will be fully enveloped in power.

## — 2 —

When you are fully enveloped in power, then you are inwardly solid and stable. When you are inwardly solid and stable, then no one can stand up to you. When no one can stand up to you, then you can divide people's power and divert their momentum, as if you were their god.

## — 3 —

Take the empty by solidity, take the lacking by having, like using pounds to weigh against ounces; then movements will surely be followed, initiatives will surely find cooperation. Bending a single finger, you observe the rest in order; setting changes in motion, you see how they take shape. No interloper can get in your way.

## — 4 —

When you are thoroughly versed in how initiatives draw cooperative response and use stealth to spot interlopers, then it is clear how to set changes in motion, and thus power can be divided.

## — 5 —

When you are going to set changes in motion, it is imperative first to nurture the will and conceal intent so as to espy gaps, leaks, and interlopers.

## —6—

Those who know to stabilize solidity nurture themselves; those who make themselves deferential nurture other people. So when the spirit is there, armaments disappear. Then you give shape to trends in a constructive and beneficial manner.

## E. Dispersing momentum: the method is modeled on a bird of prey

## —1—

Dispersing momentum is an operation of the spirit. To do this, it is necessary to act in pursuit of openings. When your forcefulness is fully developed within, if you figure out gaps and deploy that forcefulness, then momentum can be dispersed.

## —2—

Those who can disperse momentum keep their mind empty and open and their will full to overflowing. If intent deteriorates and forcefulness is lost, the vital spirit is not focused, and one's speech is irrelevant and erratic.

## —3—

Therefore you observe people's will and intent in order to calculate measures for them: then you use logic to persuade them and plan things, making full use of adaptation and convention, and balancing weaknesses and strengths.

— 4 —

If there is no gap, then you will not disperse momentum. To disperse momentum, await an opening to move, so that when you go into action the momentum of [opposing] force is split.

— 5 —

To be skilled at seeking out gaps, it is necessary to inwardly refine the five energies and outwardly observe emptiness and fullness, not losing the solidity to split and disperse [opponents] when going into action. Then movements follow your will, and you know the underlying strategies.

— 6 —

Momentum is a determining factor of gain or loss, a force in strategic change. Those whose momentum gets dispersed are those who have not been watching with the carefulness of the spirit.

### F. Transforming freely: the method is modeled on a predatory beast

— 1 —

Transforming freely means inexhaustible strategy. To be inexhaustible, it is necessary to have the mind of a sage, thereby getting to the source of unfathomable knowledge, and using unfathomable knowledge to master mental arts.

## —2—

Thereby the spirit and the Way merge into one: discerning myriad types by changes, you can expound principles inexhaustibly.

## —3—

Strategies and plans have individual forms: they may be adaptable or definitive, covert or overt, lucky or unlucky. The types of undertakings involved are not the same. Therefore sages take this to heart and use the capacity of transforming freely to seek what is appropriate.

## —4—

Therefore those who participate in creative activity, in performing initiating actions, always embrace the Great Way to observe the realm of spiritual light. Heaven and earth are infinite, human affairs are inexhaustible: in each case you see the appropriate planning in terms of what will successfully complete that type of affair. Then one will know whether it will be auspicious or inauspicious, and whether it will end up in success or failure.

— 5 —

Those who transform freely may turn to good luck, or they may turn to bad luck: sages use the Way to foresee survival and destruction, and then know to turn freely but follow the right direction.

— 6 —

Free adaptation is the basis of harmonizing words; right direction is the basis of managing affairs. Transformation is the basis of examining plans. Dealing with people is the basis of examining intentions behind advance and retirement. For all of them you must see what is fitting in order to sum up the essential and communicate coherently.

### G. Focusing the mind's eye: the method is modeled on psychic divination

— 1 —

Focusing the mind's eye is for determining impending perils. Events have natural courses, people have successes and failures: it is imperative to examine movements signaling impending perils.

— 2 —

Therefore sages await virtuous people without artificial contrivance; they examine the content of their discourse and assign them to appropriate tasks.

— 3 —

The mind's eye is knowledge, focus is practical action. When sages focus on something and talk about it, if there is something inappropriate, they will not express it in words.

— 4 —

So wise people do not miss what others say just because they themselves can speak. Therefore their rhetoric is not prolix; and their hearts are not empty, their wills are not deranged, and their intentions are not evil.

— 5 —

Only when they have confronted the degree of difficulty do they devise strategy for it; they consider it fruitful to follow the natural course.

— 6 —

When they can stop opponents from adapting and can unsettle their order, this is called great achievement.

— 7 —

If they add anything or subtract anything, in each case they express it in words.

## —8—

Use tactics that divide power and disperse momentum in order to see the mind's eye of others. Threaten their vulnerabilities and you can be sure about them.

## —9—

Skillful focus of the mind's eye is like splitting open a ten thousand-foot dam and letting the water gush out, like rolling round boulders into a valley ten thousand feet deep: the ability to carry this out is a matter of formation and momentum making it have to happen thus.

# HOLDING THE PIVOT

— 1 —

HOLDING THE PIVOT REFERS to production in spring, growth in summer, harvest in autumn, and storage in winter. This is the order of Nature, which is not to be opposed; those who oppose it inevitably fail even if they have some success.

— 2 —

Therefore human leaders also have a natural pivot, producing, growing, harvesting, and storing, which is also not to be opposed; those who oppose it inevitably decline, even if they flourish. This Way of Nature is the overall guideline for human leaders.

# COURSE FROM THE CENTER

## — 1 —

THE COURSE FROM THE CENTER means helping those in distress and attending to emergencies. Intelligent and benevolent people are needed to carry this out. Those who are rescued and given support in distress never forget the favor.

## — 2 —

Intelligent people associate with the good, but are benevolent to all. Those who exercise benevolence follow the Way. And those who help out captives develop and employ small people.

## — 3 —

Generally speaking, when intellectuals find that society is abnormal and the time is dangerous, it may somehow be possible to avoid being buried; society may attack and destroy the intelligent, or it may consider immorality to be virile and heroic. They may be suppressed and condemned, they may anxiously preserve themselves, or they may establish themselves after repeated setbacks.

— 4 —

So the Way values controlling other people, not being controlled by other people. Those who control people hold the handle of power; those who are controlled by people lose their own direction.

— 5 —

This is how you make a description when you see a form; make an image of an entity to depict it; discern the tone when you hear a voice; dissolve enmity; fight antagonists; create ties with people as they part; reject speech; concentrate attention; and preserve justice.

— 6 —

To make a description when you see a form and make an image of an entity to depict it means to produce a symbolic representation. This can be grasped by influence, appearance, and image.

— 7 —

People with a discipline do not look at anything improper and do not listen to anything unorthodox. Their speech is based on classical literature; their behavior is not indecent. They take their Way for their form, and its virtues for their appearance. Their mien is dignified, their expression warm.

They cannot be captured by images. Hide your feelings, be guarded, and keep at a distance from them.

— 8 —

As for discerning the tone when you hear a voice, this means that when the moods of voices are not the same, caring does not connect. Disparate tones do not match; only the middle note, it seems, can be master of all tones.

— 9 —

When the tone is not harmonious, that means grief. For this reason, when voices scatter injury, disgrace, and destruction, their words inevitably offend the ears. Even if people like that are well known for fine deeds, it will not do to form partnerships with them. This is because their moods are not compatible, and their tones are not harmonious.

— 10 —

As for dissolving and fighting antagonists, these expressions mean resolving matters with weak enemies and fighting the strong. Having fought strong antagonists, those who attain victory become high in merit and full of power. The weak grieve over their loss and lament their lowliness, vilify their names and disgrace their clans.

## — 11 —

So when the dominant hear of merit and power, they proceed rashly and do not know when to withdraw. When the weak hear grieving over defeat and see the casualities, they fortify themselves to resist to the death. When aggressors have no great power, and defenders have no great power, both can be taken over by threat.

## — 12 —

As for creating ties with people as they part, this refers to statements that bind others to you, causing them to keep thinking of you. Thus when you deal with those who are honest and trustworthy, you praise their conduct, sharpen their will, and speak of what may be done and when you may meet again, such that they are glad. Then call on others near them for witness, to wrap up what has transpired and make your own earnest sincerity clear before letting them go.

## — 13 —

As for rejecting speech, this refers to spying out shortcomings. When words are many, they inevitably contain numerous shortcomings. Perceiving people's shortcomings, test them: shake them up by mention of taboos, and scare them by making reference to the prohibitions of the times, so that people are intimidated. After that, form a bond of trust with them to pacify their minds. Keep what they say confidential, concealing it and warning them not to reveal their own incompetence to people of many devices.

## — 14 —

As for concentrating attention, this means that when you meet people fond of learning technical arts, you praise them far and wide, test them by means of the Way, and startle them with strangeness: then people will have their attention fixed on you. Present them to society, test them against precedent, rectify their past errors, and ally yourself with those who are honest and sincere to you.

## — 15 —

If you meet people addicted to alcohol and sex, have music played to move them, worry them with the prospect of inevitable death and shortening days of life, and amuse them with things they have not seen, so that ultimately they may observe life in a broader context, enabling them to have a reconciliation.

## — 16 —

As for preserving justice, this means keeping intact with humanity and justice, and searching out what lies within hearts, in order to mesh with them.

## — 17 —

Searching hearts means finding out what rules them; by way of the external you control the internal. If matters have complicated twists and turns, you go along with them accordingly.

## — 18 —

That is why petty people imitating others will use this in a perverse and sinister way, even getting to the point where they can destroy families and usurp countries.

## — 19 —

Without wisdom and knowledge, you cannot preserve your home with justice and cannot preserve your country with the Way. The reason sages value the subtlety of the Way is truly because it can change peril into safety, rescue the ruined and enable them to survive.

# *NOTES TO*
## The Master of Demon Valley

### Opening and Closing

*"Opening and closing" means activation and deactivation, switching on and switching off.*

1. The opening and closing of yin and yang refer to the alternation of opposite or complementary trends of events or modes of behavior.

The doorway of survival and destruction refers to the critical pivot of every situation or course of affairs, the crucial point at which success or failure of adaptation spells survival or destruction. To "keep vigil at the doorway" means to watch for these key factors or moments.

The "ends and beginnings of all types" means the aims and motivations of all kinds of people, and the processes of all sorts of events.

2. The unity of the Way and the endless variety of its transformations are simultaneously manifest in the capacity of universal adaptation to any circumstances.

3. The essential point of this passage is that sages do not impose order by external fiat, but achieve order by working responsively with the pattern of actualities. Several strategic actions mentioned illustrate ways in which sages bring people's inner qualities and ideas to light, and put them to the test to see their real worth. Whatever their good and bad characteristics, whatever their strengths and weaknesses, only by accurate assessment of people can leaders manage them effectively.

4. Here opening and closing refer to the activation and deactivation of lines of communication. Again emphasis is placed upon

the need for opening and closing to be based on well-considered decisions.

5. Sages can first go along with others because of what they themselves maintain: they have their own principles and their own discipline, so they can go along with others to find out all about them without danger of losing their own purpose or compromising themselves.

When they want to open up lines of communication they value thoroughness, so that there is no confusion or misunderstanding. When they want to shut down and break off contact, they value secrecy, so that nothing leaks out.

In either case, it is best done in a subtle manner, so that confusing emotions are not aroused.

6. Shutting down is used to make sure of people's sincerity when it is necessary to see whether their loyalty or interest is based on truth or principle, or whether it is based on enthusiasm fueled by personality gratifications such as the enjoyment of giving and receiving attention.

7. Opening and closing are natural principles, observed in natural phenomena and imitated by Taoists in their physical, social, and spiritual exercises. Maneuvers characterized by "reversing" refer to strategic acts designed to reverse the mode from open to closed or vice versa: a reversal in either direction might be used to repel an attack, to cover up a weakness, or to oppose an offense.

8. Knowing when to speak and when to remain silent, what to express and what to conceal, is an essential science of "opening and closing."

9. It is instructive to note the tremendous breadth of meaning traditionally associated with yin and yang, as compared to the relative narrowness of popular Western usage, which largely follows the misapprehensions of Carl Jung on this point.

10. One speaks of good to initiate projects because it is necessary to articulate a positive purpose; one speaks of bad in order to conclude strategic planning because it is necessary to take problems into account in order to develop a comprehensive approach to undertakings.

11. To get people to accept what you say, speak to them in accord with their state of mind.

12. In the context of strategy, to be so small as to have no inside means to be so selfless and inconspicuous as to be unnoticed and unreadable, while to be so large as to have no outside means to embrace all in your field of awareness so as to apprehend the total situation and take everything into account.

Yin and yang modes are used to achieve strategic adjustments such as those mentioned here, switched on or off according to what is needed and what can be accomplished at a given time.

13. Development of the body through stillness refers to Taoist "quiet sitting," which is used for a number of purposes, including healing and tuning the internal organs.

Using yang to seek yin means enveloping with virtue in the sense of using the safety of virtue as a basis for attaining sublime rest. Using yin to crystallize yang means exercise of power in the sense of using serenity and selflessness to control and stabilize energy.

14. The round and the square refer to adaptation and regulation, two primary approaches to accomplishing undertakings. The door of the round and the square means that upon which the appropriate use of adaptation and regulation hinges. It could be called the sum total of the key elements of the situation, or it could be called the knowledge of what will work.

## Response

1. The "formless," the Tao, or Way, is the metaphysical ground of being, the matrix of natural law. The "great civilizing influence

of ancient times" refers to the Way of government and leadership, which according to Taoist belief developed from emulation of natural law. The idea that adaptation and change are inevitable and necessary in government and law was a logical consequence of this way of thinking, but it was resisted by conservative Confucians.

2. Both inward and outward stillness are techniques for listening to others without influencing what they say by your reactions. Because Asian businessmen and politicians employ these techniques as a matter of course, Westerners who do not understand what is happening tend to think they are being typical "inscrutable Orientals." One of the techniques of mind control, of course, is to make use of stereotypes to trap attention within narrow limits; by knowing how to do this, stereotypees can even take advantage of stereotypers by manipulating the resulting blindness for their own purposes.

3. To use formlessness to inquire critically into that which is voiced means to exercise the ability to look at matters from all angles by virtue of entertaining no mental fixations or attachments, which would automatically affect one's perception and understanding.

4. People may be drawn to organizations by prospects of success and reward, or they may be drawn by a sense of affinity of aims and ideals, or they may be drawn by admiration and faith. It is essential to understand the nature of the attraction in order to understand the character of those attracted.

5. To work effectively with others, particularly in a supervisory or leadership capacity, it is important to understand their mentalities so as to be able to predict their patterns of response. Skillful use of language to establish a basis of communication also demands perceptive attention to the effects of specific words and images on each individual and each group in order to evolve a workable attunement of minds and ideas.

6. Sages of all the great spiritual traditions have been known for uncanny psychic influence over other beings, including plants, animals, ghosts, and spirits, as well as fellow humans. They also developed less invisible ways of influencing the less sensitive and the more recalcitrant; these were imitated by enterprising and ambitious people, but without the inner knowledge of sages, the desired harmony could not be achieved, and so tyranny was adopted to take the place of the charisma that was lacking.

7. Listen before speaking, coil before springing, start at the beginning, sow before reaping. More of the seemingly paradoxical but actually logical Taoist tactics like those represented in this passage of *The Master of Demon Valley* are found in the *Tao Te Ching* (chap. 36), which calls this kind of strategy "subtle illumination" and explains its effectiveness by saying that "flexibility and yielding overcome adamant coerciveness."

8. The techniques taught by the Master of Demon Valley have applications for both leaders (or potential leaders) and those who are working (or may be considering working) with or for them.

9. This passage sums up the importance of discerning observation in managing people. The classic *Book of Change* says, "Overseeing by knowledge is appropriate for a great leader." It also says, "Attentive overseeing is auspicious and impeccable."

10. Equanimity and calm are needed for objectivity in assessing people, lest perceptions be distorted by temporary emotions. Even if you reject some things, it is important to understand them, because your rejection does not mean you will not have to deal with them or their consequences. Serenity and detachment are needed to gain objective understanding, not only of that which touches off obvious aversion or attraction, but also of that which seems relatively neutral and therefore does not set off such a clear signal of the need to examine one's opinions.

11. If you do not know yourself you cannot really know others, because you have no way to gauge the effect of unconscious subjective bias on your thought and perception. This is why Ch'an Buddhists, for example, used to insist on the absolute necessity of self-enlightenment before attempting to teach others. *The Art of War* says, "If you know others and know yourself, you will not be imperiled in a hundred battles" (chap. 3, "Planning a Siege").

12. To guide in a "round" or "rounded" way means to be flexible and ready to adapt; this is necessary "before you can see formations," when things are indefinite. To employ people "squarely" or "with rectitude" means to employ them in a just and reasonable manner, according to mutually recognized principles and standards; this is possible "once formations have taken shape" and it becomes clear just who is who and what is what.

13. The *Tao Te Ching* says, "Very great leaders are only known to exist" (chap. 17). The purposes of revealing no obvious form and maintaining privacy are to thwart interlopers, baffle would-be flatterers, and prevent mechanical routine from usurping the throne of real knowledge and compromising the ability to adapt to changing actualities in a sensitive and creative way.

## ACCEPTANCE AND SOLIDARITY

1. Those who are on friendly terms in spite of distance are those who may have different histories and be in different situations yet spontaneously share similar outlooks and ideals, or people whose relationship is not essentially based on outward personality but on inner character. Those who are alienated in spite of closeness are personal or professional associates whose natures are not in psychological or spiritual harmony in spite of existing social and/or political alliances.

2. Someone who shows every sign of willingness to cooperate

and be of service may be rejected, if the leader can see that this individual is really serving personal ambition and will therefore eventually betray the greater good. Someone who is unwilling to work for a government or organization, in contrast, may by this very act of conscience open the eyes of would-be employers to dysfunction in the working environment that would thwart the best intentions and efforts of even the most intelligent and able individuals.

It is related that one of the Sufi saints of thirteenth-century Spain who had the habit of denouncing tyrants regardless of possible consequences to himself was on one occasion imprisoned at the command of the grand vizier and sentenced to death. Brought up before the ruler for review, as was customary with cases involving capital punishment, the Sufi was asked if he had retained his belief in the unity of God. The Sufi recited some verses of sacred Recital and expounded their meanings to the sultan, who was so impressed that he asked the Sufi to join his court. At this the saint began to laugh at the ruler, telling him to go to hell, denying his right to rule, and venting his wrath upon the corrupt and decadent nobles and aristocrats of his court. Seeing that he couldn't hire the Sufi, the ruler presented him with gifts and a pardon. The saint accepted the pardon, returned the gifts, and went on his way. The grand vizier, meanwhile, who had been trying to get rid of the Sufi for a long time because he exposed the faults and evils of the powerful people of the time, was himself removed for his villainy and put to death.

3. Taoist manuals of leadership place particular emphasis on looking for talent in unknown places, in consideration of the fact that most of the self-seeking pretenders to knowledge are easily visible as they crowd around potential employers. The great strategist, general, and statesman Zhuge Liang of second-century China wrote, "For strong pillars you need straight trees; for wise

public servants you need upright people. Straight trees are found in remote forests; upright people come from the humble masses. Therefore when rulers are going to make appointments they need to look in obscure places" (*Mastering the Art of War*, "The Way of the General: Pillars of State").

4. Virtue can be interpreted to mean worthy and laudable qualities, or charismatic power, or even character in general, whatever it may be. Ties made by virtue may thus refer to bonds cemented by such feelings as admiration, trust, or the fascination of charisma; or to the general feeling of commonality and familarity sensed among people of similar character. Ties made by partisanship are commonplace bonds of mutual association involving sharing of agreements and conventions identifying that association. Ties made by money are also commonplace and may take many forms, from business arrangements to gifts and bribes. Ties made by sex range from political, social, and/or economic ties formed by marriage and concubinage to circles of personal and political influence cemented by gifts and bribes using sexual favors as a medium of exchange.

5. In the context of strategic arts, "going by others' wishes" is an application of the principle enunciated in the *Tao Te Ching*, "If you want to take, first you must give" (chap. 36). The idea is that in order to see what people have to offer in the way of ideas and abilities, and in order to discover what people really want and need, the best method is to go along with them for a while, becoming an emptiness to their fullness in order to elicit expression of what is within them, without distorting or deflecting anything by your own projections or reactions, like becoming silent to listen.

6. This passage depicts the hidden mastery of the sage going along with others selflessly in order to find out what they can do

and what they need for the fulfillment of their lives. No one can see what the sage is doing at the time, like the spider leaving no traces. Therefore the sage is left to operate freely and see things as they are in themselves, without the interference of others' contrived opinions and devices, such as are always forthcoming "once formations are evident."

7. "Those who wish to be convincing strive to make their calculations in secret" because strategy without freedom to maneuver unexpectedly can hardly be effective. *The Art of War* says, "The formation and procedure used by the military should not be divulged beforehand" (chap. 1, "Strategic Assessments").

8. Threats and promises from a human source of authority are not as powerful as informed understanding of perils and possibilities. The skill of leadership in this case is to present principles and facts in a manner consistent with the interests of those in their charge.

9. Taoist teachings emphasize the importance of timing in all affairs, be they political, professional, or spiritual. The *Book of Change*, when read in a Taoist manner, is all about times and timing, showing how to meet each situation with an appropriate manner of response.

10. Internal contradictions can thwart measures even if they seem right for the external time. Therefore it is important to examine the structure of undertakings and establishments in themselves, as well as in terms of their coherence within the overall context in which they are expected to operate.

11. When speaking of the past, conventional terms are used at first (before the "bonding" of parties has been effected) in order to avoid creating useless emotional upset by contravening customarily accepted views of history. Adaptable words, such as abstract principles or general patterns, are used to speak of the future, so

that they can accommodate the broadest possible range of contingencies and still retain useful and meaningful coherence.

12. This is a typically Taoist description of how sages are said to govern: not by trying to impose their own personal wills upon the national polity and the masses of the people, but by determining what is already there and skillfully arranging existing facts and forces such as they are in working relations designed to bring out the optimum efficiency and advantage possible under any circumstances. Thus in order to govern people, sages need to guide and direct them; to guide and direct people, sages need to know their aims and hopes; to know their aims and aspirations, sages need to watch what people undertake of their own accord.

13. Disharmony means something is unknown, because it is more the lack of knowledge, rather than the possibly sinister nature of the "something" itself, that makes constructive adaptation impossible. "Better the devil you know . . ." is one reflection of this principle.

"When there is collusion but not solidarity, there is overt alliance but covert alienation." The ability to discern this in opponents is half of victory.

14–15. These passages resume the idea of different combinations of intimacy and alienation introduced in the first paragraph of this chapter. The intervening passages have been dealing with specific principles of relationships; the concluding passages first summarize the extreme poles of working relationships, then turn to the use and purpose of this understanding.

16. This paragraph resumes the ideas introduced in paragraph 3.

17. A Ch'an Buddhist classic says, "When you meet a swordsman, draw your sword; do not recite poetry to one who is not a poet."

18. When you understand the mechanisms of formation and dissolution of relationships, you can employ them at will. In this context, relationships include those between or among individuals, and those between individuals or groups and the total context of events. Thus your actions can be successful if you can predict the reactions they will evoke; you can also use this knowledge to avoid or prevent action. The key point emphasized is to get the critical mechanism: the often unannounced "trial" testing the inner character of the individual is how this knowledge is used or unused.

19. Note that tyrants also have their versions of reason, virtue, humanity, justice, courtesy, and culture. Thus the Taoist sage Chuang-tzu said, "Nothing compares to using clarity."

20. Classical poetry and documents (such as would be included in the Bible, for example) provide a common ground for impersonal yet mutually meaningful discourse; thus such literature is especially useful as a matrix of conversation, in order to underline certain things without making it seem like insistence on subjective views. This device can be used to draw out others, and also to veil oneself if necessary; it can be used to clarify things to those with whom you wish to work, and also to muddle things for those whom you wish would leave you alone.

21–22. Paragraph 21 is addressed to rulers and leaders; paragraph 22 is addressed to administrators and advisors.

"If the leadership is self-satisfied and pays no attention to what outsiders have to say, then laud it to the skies." People in positions of authority who are self-satisfied cannot hear anything but praise: so crafty advisors first get their attention by praise, then gradually sneak in advice on the "praise channel," making it seem to the otherwise heedless rulers like they thought of it themselves.

23. The *Tao Te Ching* says, "The great image has no form, the

Way hides in namelessness; only the Way can lend and perfect" (chap. 41). It also says, "It produces but does not possess; it acts without presumption, it fosters growth without ruling: this is called hidden Virtue" (chap. 51).

## STOPPING GAPS

1. The near at hand is unseen when you only regard superficial appearances or strategic projections, and do not examine the underlying premises and intentions of what is said. The remote can be known when you heed the lessons of past events in order to predict the course of future events. The best-known and least effective version of the practice of "questioning the past to discern the future" is looking for someone or something to blame. The least-known and most effective version is seeking to find out what actually happened, how, and why, in order to obtain an intelligent understanding of causes and effects.

2. Different ways of closing a gap are used according to the nature of the opening. There may be countless variations, but some essential defensive or remedial tactics might be defined in general terms. A gap caused by a defect or deficiency is "shored up." A gap caused by the intrusion of alien elements is "repelled." A gap caused by inefficient or counterproductive activity is "stopped." A gap caused by an accidental or inherent weakness is "hidden." A gap caused by a temporary breakdown in defense mechanisms is "overwhelmed." The expression "stopping gaps" can in some cases also be read, "striking gaps," in which case it represents offensive strategy (in contrast to preventative and defensive strategy).

3. Here the essentially preventative and defensive nature of the art is made clear. Offensive maneuvering (striking gaps), from this point of view, is legitimate only in the sense that surgery is a legitimate way to remove a malignant growth in order to restore

the balance and harmony of the whole system. The *Book of Change* devotes particular attention to advice on these seven skills of personal success and leadership: preserving oneself in times of peril, clarifying things as they happen, mastering strategy, discerning the subtle, starting from slight beginnings, working against long odds, and nipping problems in the bud.

4. Early Taoist texts such as *Huainan-tzu* (see *The Book of Leadership and Strategy*) and *Wen-tzu* contain many diagnostic descriptions of malignant social and political behavior that is actually aberrant yet in fact the norm under certain conditions of ignorance and alienation.

5. The methods of "plugging gaps" noted here were expounded by followers of other philosophies, but the Taoists held the view that no particular method could be regarded as a fixed standard or unconditional imperative. The criterion of political orthodoxy, therefore, was seen by Taoists as a matter of effect rather than an issue of dogma.

6. Closing gaps is a means of "effecting a restoration." Opening gaps is a means of "effecting an overthrow."

7. "Sages are servants of heaven and earth," not of their own personal ambitions or their own party's agenda. This is not a moral injunction; it is simply a working definition of a "sage."

## EXCITATION AND ARREST

1. People of intelligence and ability will more likely be attracted to those who can in fact fairly judge them, because that is the most efficient way for both parties to make positive use of their perception and their talents. Charlatans and adventurers with private agendas are drawn to rich and powerful idiots, not to those who can see what is what.

2. To discern sameness and difference means to gain a thorough

and detailed understanding of whatever is of concern, to see through superficial similarities and differences in order to determine what harmonizes with what, who is in tune, and who is on a separate line.

3. The idea is to get to know what kind of brains and abilities are around, and what kinds of problems need to be addressed; then it is possible to go into effective action, after a truthful assessment of the relevant human and material factors.

4. "Hooking and clamping" means grabbing attention (or emotion) and fixating it on something. Excitation makes the brain more sensitized and susceptible to being "grabbed," and the experience of unconscious association causes one thus "grabbed" to be "arrested" (fixated) on the source of the excitement, or on something or someone perceived to be associated with or representative of that source. Professional advertising, including that branch of this industry specifically involved in political campaigning, has recognized and practiced this principle with enormous effect.

5–10. These and other strategies are also discussed in *Huainantzu* and *Mastering the Art of War*.

## OPPOSITION AND ALLIANCE

2. The point of "clarifying terms" is to establish an open, public standard by which public affairs can be measured and discussed. Specifically, the purpose is to make it impossible for pedagogues and politicians to distort public perceptions by habitual abuse of language (such as speaking exclusively in emotionally charged but otherwise vacuous clichés).

3. "The world has no fixed values." This statement, which is an observation anyone who lives more than a few decades can confirm in some sense, also has no fixed value. Here it means that

sages do not arbitrarily impose on the world; as servants of heaven and earth, they "do nothing" for personal profit, yet "there is nothing they do not effect" when it is necessary to do so in order to maintain or restore the balance and harmony of the world.

4. The first sentence of this paragraph is a statement of the criterion for fairness and equitable justice in social policy. When fairness is lacking, then it is necessary to restore balance. The rest of this paragraph outlines the abstract principle of herding factions onto an open ground of objectivity and equal justice, discouraging bias and encouraging fairness.

5. If accurate evaluation is key to success in promoting fairness and justice, then fairness and justice are key to accuracy in evaluation.

7. Yi Yin was a Taoist man of knowledge who helped King T'ang found the Shang dynasty in the eighteenth century B.C.E. King Chieh was the last king of the Hsia dynasty preceding the Shang. Lu Shang was a Taoist man of knowledge who helped King Wen found the Chou (Zhou) dynasty in the late twelfth century B.C.E.

## FIGURING OUT PSYCHOLOGICAL CONDITIONS

1. For material on Taoist character analysis, see *Mastering the Art of War*, "The Way of the General," and *Vitality, Energy, Spirit*, "On Human Characters."

2–3. See also Sun Tzu, *The Art of War*, "Strategic Assessments."

4. This paragraph cites another critical piece of psychological knowledge that is put to use today with tremendous effect.

5. The classical strategic device of inscrutability is like a two-edged sword; it can cut both ways.

## PRESSURING

Most of the content of this chapter bears a close affinity to the teachings of the Taoist sages Lao-tzu and Chuang-tzu. See *The Essential Tao* and *Wen-tzu*.

## ASSESSMENT

1. "When you persuade people, you take your material from them," in that persuasion is accomplished by suiting, or appearing to suit, the ideas and feelings of others.

8. See Chuang-tzu, "The Human World."

12. Coercive agencies may use what appears to be reason or logic to induce emotional states, rendering the people thus influenced the more susceptible to specific types of suggestions and directions.

16. "When it comes to rhetoric, what is important is to be exceptional," insofar as the purpose of rhetoric is to capture attention and focus it on a specific point. The repetition of familiar slogans and clichés reinforces previously accepted conventions and convictions, but it also tends to lull the brain into a semi-automatic quasi trance that ultimately undermines the efficacy of the individual and group. The use of exceptional rhetoric is important when it is essential to boost perception to a new point of view.

## STRATEGIC THINKING

1. "Unexpected strategies" are unobstructed by reason of their very unexpectedness. This is the value of inscrutability.

"The perennial" is the Tao, or Way, which refers to the natural laws inherent in things. Following the Tao is the beginning of all strategy, because any effective measure needs to harmonize with the way things actually work.

3–4. These are directions illustrating how to analyze, formulate, or realign alliances according to the needs and potentials of the situation.

6. "Withdrawal gives rise to control" according to the Taoist theory of success, which states that a continued and unrelenting push for "progress" actually leads to breakdown and regression when it reaches a certain point. Those who know when to move forward and when to withdraw are the successful who master their options. Here, withdrawal does not mean regression, but a special kind of relaxation and removal, somewhat like the adjustment of a cooking soup from a preliminary boil to a maturing simmer.

10. "Prove them by surrounding" means to see how people handle pressures like the experience of being hemmed in on all sides.

15. "The Way of sages is covert" in not presenting an obvious target to interlopers.

## DECISION MAKING

4. The "four things" are yin, yang, yin within yang, and yang within yin. See "Opening and Closing," para. 1 of this same text. For fuller descriptions of pragmatic functions and combinations of yin and yang, see *The Taoist I Ching* and *Awakening to the Tao*.

6. In ancient times, court oracles were customarily read by a committee of scholars, not by individual soothsayers or fortune-tellers.

## TALISMANIC SAYINGS

*These sayings are mostly traditional Taoist teachings on the qualities of leadership. See the* Huainan-tzu *for further context and detail.*

# BASIC COURSE: SEVEN ARTS OF COVERT CORRESPONDENCE

*These materials are also Taoist teachings. See* Wen-tzu *for further lessons in this vein.*

## A. INVIGORATING THE SPIRIT

1. For the "five energies" see "Invigorating the spirit," paragraph 7, and "Solidifying intent," paragraph 5. Also see *Understanding Reality*, II.17, and *The Inner Teachings of Taoism*, "On the Firing Process."

7. The "five energies" in this context are will, thought, spirit, and character, as named here, plus the basic energy of mind.

## C. SOLIDIFYING INTENT

3. Here again the defensive or preventative function of inscrutability is stressed. "Acquired" means artificial or unnatural; acquired moods or energies disturb the original equilibrium of the mind, thus causing an overflow or spilloff of feelings that is perceptible, subject to manipulation, and therefore hazardous to the one so affected.

5–6. See *Tao Te Ching*, chaps. 10, 47.

## D. DIVIDING POWER

1. Dividing power refers to defensive diversion and dilution of enemy powers.

2. The total concentration and unity of "being enveloped in the spirit" is needed insofar as "dividing power" is like driving a wedge into a gap; the wedge has to be solid and "pointed." The next section, entitled "Dispersing Momentum," pursues the same general type of maneuver, but from the angle of offensive tactics.

## F. TRANSFORMING FREELY

2. "Discerning myriad types by changes" is the purpose of the *I Ching* or "Book of Change," which analyzes the proportions and

balances of forces that produce and guide changes in relationships, activities, and events.

6. "Transformation is the basis of examining plans" because plans cannot be judged as if they were applied to static situations, but must be seen as also being themselves participating factors in the evolution of ongoing situations. Their function and value have to be considered in the context of the processes in which they participate.

G. FOCUSING THE MIND'S EYE

2. There is a saying that virtuous people can be awaited but not sought. See *The Master of the Hidden Storehouse* for a fuller explanation.

4. "Wise people do not miss what others say just because they themselves can speak." This bit of wisdom applies to every department of life, not just matters of leadership.

9. At the conclusion of the chapter "Force," in *The Art of War*, Sun Tzu says,

> "Letting the force of momentum work is like rolling logs and rocks. Logs and rocks are still when in a secure place, but roll on an incline; they remain stationary if square, they roll if round. Therefore, when people are skillfully led into battle, the momentum is like that of round rocks rolling down a high mountain—this is force."

HOLDING THE PIVOT

See *Tao Te Ching*, chap. 32.

COURSE FROM THE CENTER

This chapter might be described as a Taoist course on uses of the mainstreams of current thought, including Confucian idealism, Legalist pragmatism, and Taoist psychology and strategic arts.

# The master of the hidden storehouse

# PRESERVING THE WAY INTACT

THE MASTER OF THE Hidden Storehouse lived for three years on the south face of Feather Mountain, during which time there was no sickness among the local folk, and the grain crops ripened regularly. The people privately said to one another, "When the Master of the Hidden Storehouse first came, we were surprised and thought him strange. Now we find our yearly income to be more than enough even though our daily income seems insufficient: could it be that he is a sage? Why don't we pray to him, and make a shrine to propitiate him?"

When the Master of the Hidden Storehouse heard about this, he appeared uneasy. A disciple tried to induce him to go along, but the Master said, "I have heard that people of ultimate attainment live independently in humble cottages, while ordinary people, in frantic madness, do not know where to go. Now the people of Feather Mountain are talking among themselves about propitiating me by ceremony—am I the man to be their target? This is why I am uneasy, considering the words of Lao-tzu."

The disciple said, "I disagree. A small pond has no room

for a huge fish to swim around in, but a mud puppy can sport freely in it; a small hill has no place for enormous beasts to hide, but it is good for little foxes. Moreover, since the time of the ancient kings Yao and Shun it has been an established practice to honor the wise and employ the able, to invite the good and take to the beneficial; so why should the folk of Feather Mountain not do likewise? You should listen to them and let them do what they propose."

The Master said, "Oh, come now! Were Yao and Shun in the know? When a huge beast strays far from the mountains, nets and snares trap it; when a giant fish is beached, insects torment it. Therefore the abodes of birds and beasts should be in high places, and the abodes of fish and turtles should be in deep places. Now, when people who would keep their bodies and lives intact conceal themselves, they cannot be too deeply hidden or too remote.

"I tell you, the basis of great disorder has its roots in the time of Yao and Shun; and its aftermath will remain even after a thousand generations. After a thousand generations there will surely be people eating each other."

Now before the Master had even finished speaking, a certain earl in his audience became obviously uneasy; kneeling at his seat, he said, "I am getting old; how can I put aside my business to put what you say into practice?"

The Master of the Hidden Storehouse said, "Keep your physical body intact, embrace your life, don't let your thought and rumination work frantically: if you live out your years in this way, you may thereby be able to reach what I'm talking about.

"But even so, my ability is slight, insufficient to teach you. Why don't you go south and call on my teacher Lao-tzu?"

Once the Master of the Hidden Storehouse had sent the earl away, without making an explanations to the folk of Feather Mountain he made himself like a dragon in the world.

THE NATURE OF WATER is inclined to clarity, but when soil muddies it, water cannot be clear. It is in the nature of human beings to want longevity, but when things confuse human nature, people cannot live long.

Things are means of nurturing life, but many deluded people today use their lives to nurture things. Thus they do not know their relative importance.

Therefore, in matters of sound, color, and flavor, sages take what is beneficial for life and reject what is harmful to life. This is the way to preserve life intact.

If ten thousand people shoot in concert at a single target, no target will not be hit; when the disturbances of ten thousand things erode a single life, no life will not be injured.

Therefore the way sages govern myriad things is to keep their own nature intact. When nature is intact, then the spirit is intact. People in whom the spirit is intact can succeed without cogitation and hit the mark without planning. Their spiritual illumination is all-encompassing; their will stabilizes the universe; their virtue is as if heaven-sent. They may rise to become emperors, but that does not make them haughty; they may be lowly commoners, but that does not make them ignorant. These are people who keep the Way intact.

When the mind is even and straightforward, and not seduced by external things, that is called purity. If purity can be sustained for a long time, it becomes clarity. If clarity can be sustained for a long time, it becomes openness. When the mind is open, the Way abides there intact.

WHEN ONE OF THE associates of Lao-tzu passed away, the Master of the Hidden Storehouse mourned him. His apprentice said, "Everyone in the world dies—why do you mourn him?"

The Master replied, "Everyone in the world mourns; how can I not mourn?"

The apprentice said, "But mourners grieve, whereas you have never sorrowed; what about that?"

The master responded, "I have no pleasure or happiness with anyone in the world—what would bring on sorrow?

"Remove the solid, and there is liquid; remove liquid, and there is gas. Remove gas, and there is emptiness; remove emptiness, and there is the Way.

"Emptiness is the substance of the Way; tranquillity is the ground of the Way. Reason is the net of the Way; consciousness is the eye of the Way.

"The Way is the means of preserving the spirit. Virtue is the means of broadening capacity. Etiquette is the means of equalizing manners. Things are the means of supporting the body.

"In something that should be white, blackness is considered pollution; in something that should be black, whiteness is considered pollution. So how do we know what in the world is truly pure or polluted? For this reason, I do not focus solely on the purity or pollution of things.

"Those whose vision is dim mistake yellow for red and blue for gray. Now how do we know that what we call black and white would not be considered red and yellow by the perceptive? And how do we know what in the world are true colors? For this reason, I do not get lost in the colors of things.

"Those whose fondness for money is extreme do not see anything else as likable; those whose fondness for horses is extreme do not see anything else as likable; those whose fondness for books is extreme do not see anything else as likable. So how do we know what in the world is actually likable or detestable? For this reason I do not see anything to be attached to. Nothing can mix me up!"

The ruler of the state of Ch'en sent one of his grandees on an official visit to the state of Lu. One of the aristocrats of Lu said to him privately, "We have a sage in our state — do you know him?"

The grandee of Ch'en inquired, "What actually shows that he is a sage?"

The aristocrat of Lu replied, "He is able to still his mind and yet use his body."

The grandee of Ch'en said, "Although my humble state is small, we also have a sage; but he is different from the one you mention."

The aristocrat of Lu asked, "Who is that sage?"

The grandee of Ch'en answered, "Someone named the Master of the Hidden Storehouse, who is foremost of those who have attained the Way of Lao-tzu. He can see with his ears and hear with his eyes."

When Lord Ting of Lu heard about this, he considered the Master unusual. He had the aforementioned aristocrat return the visit to Ch'en and invite the Master of the Hidden Storehouse to the state of Lu, where he would be treated with the highest honor.

When the Master arrived at the court of Lu, he was received in the Lord's private quarters. The Lord of Lu questioned him in a humble manner, and the Master explained, "I can see and hear without using my eyes and ears; I cannot exchange the functions of eye and ear. Your informant was exaggerating."

The Lord of Lu exclaimed, "Who is like you? I am even more amazed. What is your Way? I really want to hear about it."

The Master of the Hidden Storehouse said, "My body is merged with mind, my mind is merged with energy, my energy is merged with spirit, my spirit is merged with nothingness. If there is the smallest object or the slightest sound, no matter how far away they are, they are as close as the space between my eyebrows and eyelashes. Whatever comes to me, I know it completely. And yet I do not know if this is sensed by my senses or limbs, or if it is known by my internal organs or conscious thought—apparently it is just spontaneous knowing."

# APPLYING THE WAY

*N*

HEAVEN CANNOT BE TRUSTED, earth cannot be trusted; humanity cannot be trusted, mind cannot be trusted: only the Way can be trusted. How can intelligent rulers and outstanding scholars know this?

In ancient times, Chieh believed that Heaven had given him authority over the land; but since he did not apply himself to the Way, Heaven took his country away from him and gave it to the Yin dynasty. Chau also believed that Heaven had given him authority over the land; but he did not apply himself to the Way, so Heaven took his country away from him and gave it to the Chou dynasty.

Nowadays, lazy farmers believe the fruitfulness of the earth produces all grains, and they do not work on their Way: so earth deprives them of their crops and devastates them.

The Lord of Ch'i believed in human nature: he was courteous and deferential, but did not understand the Way clearly; he entrusted his whole realm to others, and they were in fact so greedy and rapacious that they took possession of his domain.

Whenever people fail to practice the Way and instead follow their minds obediently, calculations and desires proliferate, so troubles and afflictions act collectively to damage the body and reduce the life span. It is the mind that has injured them.

This is why it is said that only the Way can be trusted. Heaven and earth could not endure but for the Way. The common people cannot be orderly without the wise; government cannot be reasonable without the capable.

People who apply the Way do not reveal their function, but the blessings enrich all beings; they make nothing of their achievements, but secretly help others with unobtrusive efforts: and the common people think it happens to them naturally. Spiritually effective, work flourishing, ethereal joy endures forever.

To know this discursively is called perception; to know this nondiscursively is called the Way. Perception is used to govern people; the Way is used to stabilize people.

Going to work at dawn, toiling under the sun, sweat dripping on the ground—this is the Way of farmers.

Picking up from below, taking from above, sharpening the mind, thinking diligently, concentrating thoroughly, seeking beneficial profit—this is the Way of merchants.

Absorbing energy to nurture the spirit, detaching from thought and rumination, transcending the world, rising lightly above it, taking in the vitality of the sun, and cultivating spiritual immortality—this is the Way of the highest intellectuals.

Detaching from emotions in order to think straight, devoting full attention to the principles of order for which they work, tirelessly planning so as to successfully manage their positions—this is the Way of public servants.

Purifying the mind, eliminating subjective thoughts, examining and testing close associates, diligently seeking the talented and the worthy to bring peace and security to all people—this is the Way of leaders.

When you class them in this manner, each follows its order: if they do their work steadily without a change of heart, then it is said that the land is imbued with the Way.

Exercise the physique, and the body will remain intact; pare away emotional desires, and the spirit will remain intact; be careful of your speech, and blessings will remain intact. Keeping these three things intact is called purity and goodness.

When you are full of the Way and virtue, then ghosts and spirits will help you. When your truthfulness and justice are rich, then cultivated people will cooperate with you. When your courtesy and righteousness are complete, then ordinary people will embrace you.

Those who are perceptive affirm themselves; those who are not perceptive also affirm themselves. Those who are imbued with the Way are calm and quiet; those who are ignorant and dull are also calm and quiet. There are certainly things that seem to be right but are wrong, and things that seem to be wrong but are right.

Those who lament at first may laugh later on; what starts out auspiciously may end up unfortunately. A person may be approachable, yet have talents that cannot be approached; one may have respectable talents, yet be unworthy of respect as a person.

When respect is extreme, then there is no familiarity; when familiarity is extreme, then there is no respect. People may distance themselves from you when you approach them, and they may approach you when you distance yourself from them. When favor is extreme, then resentment arises; when there is too much love, then hatred comes about.

In some cases, speed is valuable; in some cases, slowness is valuable. In some cases, directness is valuable; in some cases, indirectness is valuable. In all affairs, the reasons for what is appropriate are very subtle, but it is imperative to know them. This is why the wise consider it difficult.

When calm, the spirit is effective. When in straits, the will is effective. When one's rank is high, one's words are effective. When one is wealthy, one's person is effective. It is the course of nature that makes this so.

Those on the same path care about each other, while those with the same skill envy each other. Those who give the same things care about each other, while those who take the same things envy each other. Those who suffer the same illness care about each other, while those who are similarly robust envy each other. This is how human feelings naturally are.

Those who are very talented yet cleave to modesty, those who are poor and lowly yet do not flatter anyone, those who labor yet do not consider that disgrace, and those who are noble and rich yet all the more respectful and diligent—such people may be said to be imbued with virtue.

# THE WAY OF GOVERNMENT

PEOPLE HAVE NO WAY to know how cold or hot the four seasons will be, or the courses of the sun, moon, stars, and planets. If they knew precisely how cold or hot the seasons were going to be, and how the celestial bodies would course, then all living beings would find their proper places and be secure in their productive activities.

Public servants also have no way to know how the rulers will distribute rewards and punishments, entitlements and emoluments. If they knew just how the rulers will distribute rewards and punishments, entitlements and emoluments, then everyone near and far, worthy and unworthy, would employ their talents and powers to the fullest in order to serve usefully.

When trust is complete, the world is secure. When trust is lost, the world is dangerous. When the common people labor diligently and yet their money and goods run out, then contentious and antagonistic attitudes arise, and people do not trust each other.

When people do not trust each other, this is due to unfairness in government practices. When there is unfairness in government practices, this is the fault of officials. When officials are at fault, penalties and rewards are unequal. When penalties and rewards are unequal, this means the leadership is not conscientious.

Now, when the leadership is conscientious, then penalties and rewards are uniform. When penalties and rewards are uniform, then officials obey the law. When officials obey the law, then order reigns. When order reigns, the common folk find their places and interact trustingly.

So we know that when the people do not trust each other, it is because the leadership is not conscientious.

The Master of the Hidden Storehouse lived in the state of Chou for five years. The king of Chou sent one of his nobles to him with a gift of silk and jewels, extending an invitation to the court of Chou.

The king said to the Master, "I am an insignificant person, lacking in virtue, a disgrace to the throne. The weather here has become irregular, with wet and dry spells at the wrong times, causing the people to suffer. How can I clear up this problem?"

The Master of the Hidden Storehouse said to the king of Chou, "Flooding is a yin disturbance. In government, yin typifies punishment; in social matters, yin typifies personal bias. Drought is an excess of yang. In government, yang typifies reward; in social matters, yang typifies plenitude.

"It seems to me that whenever there is a flood or a

drought, the rulership should rectify punishments and rewards, the officials should eliminate personal biases and beware of excess. Then corresponding problems will disappear, and a hundred blessings will arrive day by day."

AMONG THE TREASURES OF the state of Cheng were a magnificent gem and a mighty bow from foreign lands. When at some point Cheng had lost political party with the state of Hsing, the latter demanded the gem and bow from the former, on pain of armed attack.

The ruler of Cheng, disturbed by this, went to see the Master of the Hidden Storehouse. The ruler said to the Taoist sage, "The gem and the bow were obtained from foreign lands by a past ruler of Cheng and have been passed on through generations as hereditary emblems of achievement.

"Now Hsing is taking advantage of its size to demand them, threatening my state with armed aggression otherwise. What I want to do at this point is take them another gem and bow; how would that be?"

The Master of the Hidden Storehouse said, "Please calm down a bit, sir. As a matter of fact, I also have treasures here, but to display my treasures and thereby occur the blame of a ruler is something I cannot do.

"You should hand over the real things. Hsing is now using a small mistake as an excuse for putting on airs of authority and behaving in an arbitrary and dishonest manner, ravaging its allies. It will lose the loyalty of the lords.

"At this point, it is a matter of the lords hearing about this, so that they can be alerted and urged to take precautions. Let them cooperate as equals, with diligence and intelligence, and higher justice will be preserved intact. Cheng will be a leader; just wait a while. Will that not be felicitous?"

So the ruler of Cheng took the foreign gem and bow to Hsing. Before he reached the capital, however, the people of Hsing had already heard about what had transpired. They said, "The ruler of Cheng is employing the advice of a sage. How can we take these treasures and thus expose our iniquity to the world, and cause the lords concern? Let's return the goods right away and treat Cheng better."

THE HUMAN CONDITION IS to want to live and hate to die; to want security and dislike insecurity; to want glory and despise disgrace. When people get what they want, then they are happy; and when they are happy, then they are at peace. When people do not get what they want, then they are miserable; and when people are miserable, then they are insecure.

If leaders indulge their own desires, then officials and functionaries all extend their desires. If officials and functionaries all extend their desires, then everyone is affected:

the poor are drained of their labor, the rich are drained of their wealth, and society loses its order; all people fail to obtain what they want.

When people fail to obtain what they want, then they band together for protection and flee into concealment and vagrancy, gathering wild fruits to live on. The police also pursue and arrest them. Thus the insecurity and misery of the people is unbearable; so mobs gather and rebelliousness grows. If there is mobbing and rebellion, then the state is no more.

Do not be greedy for population, or the common people will run from you. Do not build huge castles and moats, or the common people will tire of you. When taxes are unfair, the poor grow poorer day by day. When punishments and awards are arbitrary and discriminatory, the rich grow richer day by day. When regulations and prohibitions are not observed in practice, then the state crumbles.

If officials and functionaries lack ability, they lose the proper measure of leniency and sternness. They may even struggle with the common people for their own profit and advantage. Because of this, craft and deceit arise, which make people treacherous and unpredictable.

Now then, when the ruled are unpredictable, the rulers are suspicious; and when the rulers are suspicious, the ruled increase in confusion. Once the ruled are confused, the officials weary of their tasks. When officials weary of their tasks, then awards are not adequate for motivation, and punishments are not adequate for deterrence. It is easy to cause a stir, hard to bring calm. This state of affairs is due to failure to find the right people for office.

The most essential thing in the art of government is to screen personnel. If people have the talent and conduct to harmonize a village, let them govern a village. If people have the talent and conduct to harmonize a county, let them govern a county. If people have the talent and conduct to harmonize a province, let them govern a province. If people have the talent and conduct to harmonize a state, let them govern a state. Only then is it possible to eliminate disaffection among the educated class.

When people do wrong in their villages, then they are to be admonished by their villages. If they do not reform, and deliberately do wrong, then they are to be beaten by county authorities. If they still do not reform, and deliberately do wrong, then they are to be exiled by the provincial authorities. If they do not reform, and deliberately do wrong, then they are to be executed by state authorities. Only thus is it possible to eliminate disruptive behavior.

When things are really done in this way, then no one in the world harbors sprouts of rebelliousness and contempt at heart. This is called bringing peace to people.

Of all the tasks of government, none is as great as finding people for public service. To prepare people for public service, nothing is as good as mastery of political science; and the best political science of all is bringing peace to people.

As far as ability to bring peace to people is concerned, generally speaking you will scarcely find 4 or 5 percent of those who have it if you test them by writing. If you test them by verbal discourse, you may find 10 or 20 percent. If you test them by psychology, behavior, and attitude, you will find a full 80 to 90 percent. This all refers, of course, to a felicitous age with a wise rulership having the clear perception and discriminating choice to make it possible.

By contrast, if it is a perilous age under an inferior rulership, if they choose people for public service by written tests, then those who indulge in artificial rhetoric show up more and more, while the upright and genuine increasingly disappear. If they choose people for public service on the basis of verbal discourse, those who are glib and superficially ornate show up more and more, while those who speak honestly and straightforwardly increasingly go into concealment. If they choose people for public service by psychological, behavioral, and attitudinal testing, then those who are outwardly upright but inwardly crooked are increasingly honored, while those who are pure, disciplined, enlightened, and genuine are increasingly obscure. In such cases, the more intellectuals get involved, the more biased government becomes; the more insistent commands become, the more disorderly people become.

A country is an enormous instrument; rulership is a serious position. If good people are found for public service, there is peace; if good people are left out, there is disorder. Leaders work hard to seek the wise and the good, and are lackadaisical about appointing ambassadors. How can those who would preserve Nature and unite humanity fail to treat good people seriously?

It is a profound disgrace for leaders when they lose the goodwill of their people. There is no more painful way to major loss of goodwill than punishment and imprisonment. When those with the power of clear understanding hear lawsuits, they may draw out the facts by pretense, or scare them out by threat, or bring them out by frankness: but even though the strategies they set up may differ, they are obliged to be impartial and fair. Thus they make it so that those who live do not feel gratitude to them, and those who die do not feel resentment toward them.

If the operation of national government, with the establishment of functionaries and maintenance of law, is done in this manner, that can be called perfect management. In an age of perfect management, the minds of the masses are harmonious and upright, all products are wholesome, and people communicate deeply with love and respect. The solidarity of upper and lower classes is unshakable, all beings are one family: even if there is some disorderly conduct or criminal misbehavior, how can that cause disturbance?

When King P'ing of the Chou dynasty restored order, once he had taken up residence in the capital he went to work looking for talented people. If he got to hear of even one example of goodness, he would be happy for days on end. The courtiers kept on telling him that there were intelligent and exceptional people among the great ministers.

Thus a year passed. The king said, "I am not enlightened in matters of virtue. While I strive to seek the wise and the exceptional, all the more it seems they run away to the wilds and will not take up public office. Why should I shut myself up listening eagerly to tales of goodness? These flattering courtiers keep on praising the great ministers to the skies; they must think I am weak and stupid, unable to determine facts clearly. They just band together, relying on each other, eventually ruining virtue by self-aggrandizement. And this is nothing yet—if I don't stop them in time, they will solidify their faction."

So the king had his three closest cabinet members executed in public, and banished five of the great ministers. He declared, "Let not those in the service of a government band with subordinates to destroy their leaders or hold onto their salaries by servile flattery."

When this was heard of throughout the land, King P'ing was lauded for impartiality and enlightenment; and seven states declared their allegiance to him.

In an age of perfect order, vehicles and clothing are plain, laws are accommodating and simple, the web of prohibitions is coarse. When vehicles and clothing are plain, then people do not struggle for the sake of envy and desire. When the laws are accommodating and simple, then the common people are not inhibited. When the web of prohibitions is coarse, then it is easy to avoid what is forbidden, and hard to transgress.

If people do not struggle for the sake of envy and desire, then their desires are few and they work at their jobs with zest. When the common people are not inhibited, then suppression is relaxed and they take pleasure in social relations. When what is forbidden is easily avoided and hard to get into, then good and bad are clearly distinct, and there is respect for virtue and a sense of conscience.

Working at your job with zest means accord. Taking pleasure in social relations means harmony. Respect for virtue and a sense of conscience means rectitude. Unstable people are incapable of accord, immoral people are incapable of harmony, dishonest people are incapable of rectitude. Accord, harmony, and rectitude constitute the basis of governing a state.

In a decadent era, vehicles and clothing are adorned elaborately, laws are many and complicated, and prohibitions are unfairly biased. When vehicles and clothing are adorned elaborately, then fashions fan the flames of desire.

When laws are many and complicated, then the common people have many inhibitions. When prohibitions are biased and unfair, then no one knows how to avoid them.

When fashions fan the flames of desire, the people are not faithful and pure: they are ashamed of simplicity and value ostentation. When the common people have many inhibitions, then feelings and aspirations are not communicated, so the relationship between the rulers and the ruled is twisted. When no one knows how to avoid the forbidden, then intrigues will repeatedly occur, and the masses will not fear death.

To be ashamed of simplicity and value ostentation is called superficiality. When the relationship between rulers and ruled is twisted, this is called obstruction. When the masses do not fear death, this is called recklessness. Truly upright people have nothing to do with superficiality, fair and honest people have nothing to do with obstruction, and capable and talented people have nothing to do with recklessness. Superficiality, obstruction, and recklessness are steps to throwing a state into chaos.

THE LORD OF HSING asked about flood and drought, order and disorder. The Master of the Hidden Storehouse said, "Flood and drought come from Nature; order and disorder come from humankind. If human affairs are harmonious and orderly, even if there are floods or droughts they cannot cause harm. That is why an ancient document says, 'When people are strong, they overcome Nature.' If human affairs are spoiled and confused, then even if there are no floods or droughts, there is daily dissolution. Do you think the downfall of ancient tyrants was only due to flood or drought?"

The Lord of Hsing bowed to the Master of the Hidden Storehouse and said, "Heaven has not abandoned me—that is why I have gotten to hear these words." Then he gave the Taoist sage ten pairs of large jewels and appointed him to an administrative post, saying, "I hope my state will be cured."

The Master of the Hidden Storehouse had no choice; camping out along the way, clad in light clothing, he fled to another land.

IN AN AGE OF PERFECT ORDER, there are no false hermits in the mountains, no dishonest profit in the markets, and no salaries for flattery at court.

One of the grandees of Cheng asked the Master of the Hidden Storehouse, "How can we get people's way of life to be pure and simple?"

The Master said, "When government is complicated and cruel, then people are unruly and deceitful. When government is sparing and unified, then people are pure and simple.

"People's mores go along with the quality of the government, like insects that take on the colors of the leaves they eat."

The grandee asked, "How can the people be enriched?"

The Master of the Hidden Storehouse said, "Tax them according to the season, have officials be pure and frugal, and the people will prosper. If taxes are levied immoderately, and officials are extravagant and indulgent, then the people will be impoverished.

"The arrows of the southeast are tipped with pure gold and fletched with eagle feathers. If used for beating, they are no different from plain sticks; but when they are shot by powerful bows in war, no one can stand up to them within a range of three hundred yards.

"There is a marvelous sword with a brilliance outshining the sun and energy greater than a violet rainbow. If used for cutting grain, it is no different from a sickle; but when it is wielded against evil, viciousness, and unrest, nothing can stop it for a thousand miles.

"There are distinctions in capacities, and there are appropriate applications. What is important is skillful accord with the time.

"When there were enlightened leaders and sage rulers in ancient times, the land was at peace, all beings flourished, and all natures attained their peak development. They skillfully adapted to the times, and were disturbed by nothing.

"More recently, the dishonest are many and the honest

are few; superficial profiteers abound, while conscientious and modest people are rare. Connivers speak out, without faith or truth. This has caused people everywhere to be suspicious and malicious toward each other. How sad it is!

"In the creation of laws, it is important to make them easy to abide by and difficult to transgress. When rectifying corruption, it is important to minimize projects and unify directives. Get rid of irresponsible behavior, and officials will be at ease. Make sure penalties are enforced, and officials will not dare to work for private personal profit. When officials dare not work for personal profit, then the common people prosper.

"The classical penal code says, 'Crimes committed by mistake are to be pardoned.' Pardon should not be repeated, for if pardon is repeated, then evil people will succeed in their schemes and ordinary people will get ideas, while the wise and the good are obstructed.

"People sometimes commit major crimes, for which they are arrested, but then they falsely implicate upright and good people, getting so many involved that they are ultimately pardoned in the interests of maintaining social order. Those who have been injured, in contrast, ultimately get no relief; all they have is their own bitterness and resentment.

"Because of this, ordinary people come to produce cunning schemes; officials are under stress, the government is cruel, and no one can put a stop to it all. This is due to the mistake of repeatedly granting pardons.

"The reason people do not like to do what is unethical or unjust is that there are penalties. The reason they strive to do what is right and just is that there are rewards. Now if the unethical and unjust are pardoned, while the ethical and just are envied and not rewarded, will it not be hard to induce people to take to goodness? If there are any intelligent leaders in the world, let them examine this thesis.

"When people are resentful, that does not mean you have nothing to do with them. When the gods are angry, that does not mean you do not worship them. When craftiness is extreme, people grow increasingly resentful; when obscene rites flourish, the gods grow increasingly angry."

# The way of leadership

WHAT ORIGINATES AND PRODUCES is Nature; what develops and completes is humanity. One who is able to nurture what Nature has produced, such that people follow along, is called a true leader.

The action of a true leader is for the purpose of keeping the energy of Nature intact; this is why officialdom is established. The establishment of officials is for the purpose of keeping life intact. Under the deluded leaders of the present age, there are so many officials as to be, on the contrary, detrimental to life, thus losing the fundamental reason for the establishment of officials.

When grass is choked, it rots; when trees are choked, they are worm-eaten; when people are choked, they become ill; when a country is choked, a hundred troubles occur at once, and danger and chaos cannot be stopped.

What it means to say that a country is choked is that the favors of the leadership do not extend to the common people, while the wishes of the common people do not come to the attention of the leadership.

Therefore, sage rulers esteem loyal ministers and upright

officers for having the courage to speak straightforwardly and cut through choking obstructions.

When rulers master themselves and return to order, then the wise and the good naturally come to them. When the king himself tills the soil and the queen herself makes cloth, the common people are spontaneously civilized.

From this point of view, the wise and the good are properly to be awaited, not to be sought. Those who are found by seeking are not sages. The common people are properly to be civilized, not to be tortured or killed; the practice of torture and execution is not true reason.

The ancient kings Yao and Shun had the diligence to be leaders, but not the desire to be leaders; thus all in the land were able to fulfill their wishes. Yao and Shun had the position of leadership, but not the ambition of leadership, so all in the land could relax.

Among the educated are those whom everyone in the land likes but the ruler dislikes; and there are those whom the ruler alone likes and everyone else dislikes. If those liked by everyone are employed, then the land is peaceful and secure; if those liked only by the ruler are employed, then the land is in peril. How can leaders indulge their personal likes and dislikes? To value those loved by the whole land, therefore, one should control one's own feelings.

The whole land includes all the beings therein; it is called a country in reference to its human population. Countries are based on people: if its people are secure, a country is secure. Therefore leaders who are concerned for their countries strive to find those who have the ability to manage people.

The reason jade is hard to distinguish is because there is another kind of stone that looks like it; the reason gold is hard to distinguish is that there is another kind of metal that looks like it. Now, if falcon feathers are pasted onto a quail, those who cannot see clearly will take it for a falcon, while those with clear vision will see it is a quail. These days there are many petty people who recite classics and esoteric writings, or study unusual arts or rhetoric: putting on elegant suits, they cause the ignorant who hear and see them to believe they are actually cultivated people. Those with understanding, however, see that they are really petty people.

Therefore, if the leadership is truly enlightened, it is reasonable to choose people based on what they say, it is reasonable to choose people based on their talents, and it is reasonable to choose people based on their actions. If the leadership is not enlightened, it is arbitrary to choose people by what they say, it is arbitrary to choose people by their talents, and it is arbitrary to choose people by their actions.

When sages employ people, they value the ability to not hear, the ability to not see, the ability to realize what cannot be said. Thus the common people are easygoing yet spontaneously orderly.

If leaders value the ability to hear, then everyone in the land will use their money and pursue profit in order to buy and sell fame and repute. If leaders value the ability to see, then everyone will seek advancement by exaggerated physical appearances and unusual arts. If leaders value the ability to speak, then everyone will adorn their words and speak glibly. Have everyone buy and sell fame and repute, compete for advancement, decorate speech, and seek distinction, and government is ruined.

Leaders all know that mirrors show what they look like, yet dislike it when educated people show what the leaders look like. The effectiveness of a mirror in showing a leader himself is small compared to the effectiveness of educated people showing a leader himself. To know the small but miss the great is ignorance.

If leaders would purify their hearts and minimize their affairs, and administrators would be respectful and frugal and mind their duties, then peace would arrive at once. And yet society seems to consider this difficult. I do not know. If the hearts of leaders are not clear and decisive, then all creatures lose the Way.

When people are picked by the ears and eyes, offices proliferate and government is confused. When people are picked by mind and thought, offices are minimized and government is pure. This is how we know that in an orderly and reasonable society effort is made to find people with abilities that cannot be seen or heard, while in a corrupt society effort is made to get people with abilities that can be seen or heard.

Do leaders know this? If people are picked by the ears and eyes, then everyone will take whatever they can get in order to buy a reputation. If people are picked by mind and thought, then everyone will strive for virtue calmly and correctly. When officials strive for virtue calmly and correctly, then people become civilized even if not told to do so. When officials take whatever they can get in order to buy a reputation, then people are not intimidated even by punishment. Do world leaders know this?

# THE WAY OF ADMINISTRATORS

WHEN A COUNTRY IS GOING to rise and flourish, the officials at court have weakness and strengths; some are repulsive, some are attractive, some are genial, some are stern, some are right, and some are wrong. When you listen to their words and observe their appearances, they seem to be dissimilar, but when you look into their aspirations and examine their hearts, you find them thoroughly dedicated to service of the nation. Therefore they are not resentful when strongly attacked, and they are not disturbed when dismissed from office. Knowing the mean, they do not deviate from reason; therefore Heaven does not confuse their timing, Earth does not diminish their gains, people do not disrupt their affairs. Ghosts and spirits sing praises, and foreign nations harmonize. Great peace being kept together, all beings develop and grow.

When a country is going to perish, the officials at court are splendidly attired, their countenances are harmonious, their speech is flowery and genteel, their movements are careful and elegant. Although the administration of a moribund country may outwardly appear to be harmonious and obedient, inwardly the officials harbor suspicions and aversions, each pursuing his own personal aims, secretly plotting each other harm. When you observe their appearance and listen to their words, they seem to be happy and harmonious, but when you look into their aspirations and examine their hearts, you will find them competing for rank. That is why they are suspicious when they hear of something unusual and startled when they see something different. Envious of each other, keeping each other in ignorance, ultimately they lose the right Way. Therefore Heaven declares disasters and Earth produces weird things. People act evilly, and ghosts and spirits cause calamities. Foreign peoples repeatedly invade, loss and chaos run rampant, and nothing develops.

When work is accomplished and government is established without ruining finances, overstraining workers, or interfering with officials, such that those below are treated well and the appreciation of the leadership is won, those who do this are loyal and wise administrators.

If they waste money, overburden people, endanger officials, take pride in temporary successes in hopes of rewards from the rulers, pay no heed to their mistakes, and leave a disastrous legacy to the nation, these are treacherous administrators.

In an age of perfect order, people are found for offices. In an age of order, offices are found for people.

The Master of the Hidden Storehouse was asked how to work for a leader. The Master said, "Once you become an administrator, your mind should be impartial, your demeanor should be harmonious, and your speech should be correct. Impartiality should not be overbearing, harmonization should not be random, and correctness should not be offensive.

"What was pure diligence in perfecting government for service of the nation in ancient times has now become pure diligence in cultivating repute in service of the self. When those who work on perfecting government for the sake of the country handle matters and clarify their reasons, their actions are appropriately suited to the totality. When those who cultivate a reputation for their own sakes handle matters and clarify their reasons, they do not understand the long run and get stuck in small measures.

"So we know that when the mind is directed by the Way, then when one encounters affairs one finds the appropriate placement. When mind is directed by affairs, then when one encounters things one misses the appropriate placement.

"If ministers in high positions do not criticize the leadership constructively, or if ministers of lesser rank are not fair, they should not be given their salaries. If the leader is not dignified and serious, and the great ministers do not show trust, then lesser ministers should not work for that court.

"The talented are not necessarily loyal, the loyal are not necessarily talented. Ministers do not worry about not being loyal; they only fear being totally loyal yet still not being trusted by the leadership. Leaders do not worry about not trusting; they only fear trusting those who cannot handle business.

"When people of higher caliber can be themselves, the world is orderly. When people of mediocre caliber can be themselves, the world is disorderly. When enlightened leaders employ people of higher caliber, they should entrust them with the authority to adapt to changes, not interfering with their actions. When they employ people of mediocre caliber, they should regulate their activities and direct them by means of rewards and punishments."

# THE WAY OF THE WISE

THE REASON WHY THE WISE and the good do not go even where they are repeatedly invited, hardly advance and easily withdraw, is not that they are so concerned about themselves that they will not die for the public good; it is just that they fear exercising utmost loyalty yet not being trusted by leaders.

Those who know themselves to have talent and perception are outwardly respectful and conscientious; thus inwardly they have no anxieties. Their relationship to the masses is correct and not contemptuous. Treated familiarly, they are all the more dignified; alienate them and they leave, yet without resentment. In desperation and danger, they ease their minds by accepting it as fate; in glory and success, they correct themselves by means of the Way.

There are those who appear to be wise, and sound as if they are wise, but on examination of their spirit and perception, they may disappoint expectation.

As for people who actually are wise, when they are in office they criticize and commend, and when out of office they maintain silence. At work, they are diligent and competent; at home, they are frugal and reserved. When they are not employed in public service, they conceal themselves among the masses, conceal their perception in their eyes, conceal their words in their mouths. Eating to their fill, they walk in peace, taking care of themselves as best they can in private, upright and unembittered.

The wise do not have doubts about events; the perceptive do not have doubts about people. People with perception are strict in their behavior, yet their demeanor is not distant; their speech is conciliatory, yet they cannot be dissuaded from reason.

Those who are worthy of the name "wise" do not call themselves wise. The test of their efficacy is in civil administration; the merit of their achievement is in managing affairs.

In a time of great peace, the best people use their perception and knowledge, mediocre people put forth all they can, and lesser people contribute their strength.

THERE WAS A MAN of Ch'i named P'ou-tzu, "The Exactor," who had the talent to manage a country, and had the discipline to be independent. He took care of his parents and was respectful to his neighbors. Considering that he was poor and had no material resources, for a long time he went around giving out truthfulness and justness. Wherever he went, few sympathized; sometimes he was ridiculed and tricked by opportunists.

Because of this, he went to the Master of the Hidden Storehouse and asked, "I have heard that perfect people forget feelings, while ordinary people cannot employ feelings constructively. Those who retain feelings strive to educate them, honoring truthfulness and justice.

"Now I consider not minding to be a skill, and regard not being trusted as being truthful. Being truthful yet not being trusted is truthfulness. Deliberate diligence aspiring to justice is considered justness, but I consider justness being just without expecting justice.

"Therefore troubles recede from the truthful and the just as long as they are always alone; how can they gain honor in their time and teach what reason places foremost?"

The Master of the Hidden Storehouse looked down, his chin to his chest, then he looked up and sighed. Serenely aloof, he began to sing:

> *When the time is positive,*
> *truth and justice shine.*
> *When the time is silenced,*
> *truth and justice hide.*
> *Positivity or silence, shining or hiding,*
> *I have no personal standpoint at all;*
> *I do not know what to say.*

"If you operate true nature in such a way as to conform to what is appropriate," the Master continued, "and yet no one responds, that means truth is not current. When truth is not current, furthermore, that is called loss of the Way.

"In times when the Way is lost, superior people hide. The reason concealment is just is that nothing can be done."

LORD CHI ASKED THE MASTER of the Hidden Storehouse, "In what way can the wise and talented be attracted?"

The Master said, "The wise should properly be awaited, not sought. Talent is there if you take care of it; if you seek it without care, it is not there.

"If the ruler is peaceful and the ministers are enlightened, if the upper classes are not exempt from punishments and the lower classes are not excluded from benefits, then wise people will come on their own to seek employment.

"When wise people are employed, all within the four seas hear with clear ears and see with clear eyes; they are even-minded and have no depression. The weather naturally fulfills its cycle, the earth is naturally peaceful, myriad beings evolve, and ghosts and spirits cannot affect anything.

"That is why it is said that the wise should properly be awaited, not sought. If personnel are sought by a ruler who is diligent and enlightened and by great ministers who are harmonious and orderly, then this will attract those who are broad-minded, magnanimous, impartial, honest, and able to bring peace and stability to the people.

"If personnel are sought by a ruler who is cruel and demanding and by great ministers who are impulsive and hasty, this will attract people who are evil-minded, opportunistic, destructive, and immoral.

"If personnel are sought by a ruler who is suspicious and by great ministers who are crafty and servile, this will attract strange people who show off weird arts.

"If personnel are sought by a ruler who considers himself wise and by great ministers fixed in their positions, this will attract superficial people who seek praise, are polluted by greed, and are ostentatious in outward display.

"If personnel are sought by a ruler who is capricious and whimsical and by great ministers who are devious and dishonest, this will attract people who are outwardly loyal but inwardly crooked, whose feelings are poison but whose words are conciliatory.

"This is why it is said that talent is there if you are careful, but not if you seek it without care.

"When ancient kings found wise ministers, it was through a scientific and logical process. When a ruler embodies the Way, exalts humaneness, spreads enlightenment, is both wise and valiant, thoughtful and congenial, brilliantly luminous, magnanimous and considerate, correct and upright, then the wise will spontaneously gather, seeking employment in public service. They are not found by selection."

Lord Chi asked, "You say that the wise will come spontaneously, without being sought. Will unwise people also come on their own, without being sought?"

The Master of the Hidden Storehouse replied, "The unwise who come on their own without being sought are sure to be numerous! When the land has the Way, then wise people spontaneously come without being sought; when the land lacks the Way, unwise people come on their own without being sought. Human leaders who have the Way are rare; human leaders without the Way are plentiful. There are few good and wise people in the world, and many unworthy people. Obviously the unwise who come on their own without being sought will be numerous."

Lord Chi asked, "The wise can certainly manage the land, and the talented can also manage the land. How do the wise and the talented differ?"

The Master of the Hidden Storehouse said, "That is a very pointed question! Those who do not pursue entitlement and honor when their work is done and their task accomplished, but are gracious and retiring, simple and frugal, are those who are called wise. Those who glory in remuneration and honor when their work is done and their task accomplished, who glorify their fulfillment of aspiration, are those who are called talented.

"The wise can keep a nation secure, the talented can keep a nation orderly. Keeping a nation secure is harmonious, peaceful, and uncontrived, so people are not aware of that power. Keeping order involves diligently taking a leading role in affairs, so people know where to attribute the credit.

"One wise person is more than able to direct many talented people, but even a multitude of talented people cannot take the measure of a single wise person.

"Such are the different domains of the wise and the talented.

"There are those who live in mountain forests yet are still clamorous; there are those who live in ordinary society yet are calm. There are those who are clamorous but upright, and there are those who are quiet but devious. People who appear to be base and vulgar yet can be sagacious are so rare as to be hardly one in ten thousand. People who are proper and elegant in appearance yet are really petty people are so common as to be fully nine out of ten.

"Those who understand writings without working on the wording, who assess measures without fussing about individual manners, who know the good regardless of whether people praise them, and who stop the bad regardless of criticism, these can be called the perceptive."

# THE WAY OF EDUCATION

MIN TZU-CH'IEN [son of a disciple of Confucius] asked Confucius, "How far apart are the Way and filial piety?"

Confucius replied, "The Way is a sublime function of Nature; filial piety is a supreme virtue in the course of human life. What envelops and operates the universe, produces and develops all beings, perfects the forms of all species, disburses nature and life, is most real in effect and is not ruled by beings, not governed by things, not controlled by effort, not accessible to the senses, and yet is there—this is called the Way.

"When this is used in the human context, it is called filial piety. Filial piety means serving your parents well. Serving your parents well is based on respect and obedience. When you are consciously receptive to them, the outward manifestation of obedience reaches everywhere. Whatever you say, whatever you think, you dare not forget your parents; with each action, each step, you dare not forget your parents. In government service, you dare not be disloyal; in association with friends, you dare not be unfaithful. In dealing with subordinates, you dare not be disrespectful. In promoting good, you dare not be lax. Even when you are alone indoors, you still dare not relax your sincerity. This is called complete filial piety.

"So filial piety is the consummation of sincerity. It reaches the spirits and illumines the land. When something is sensed, there is unfailing response; this is a result of serving your parents well.

"In ancient times, the great filial piety of the sage King Shun was such that even though his father's concubine fooled his father into attacking him repeatedly, Shun was ever more respectful and deferential, harboring no resentment. His father had him go down into a well to dig it deeper, and then had it filled in with earth. At this time, Heaven quaked its approval of Shun, and the spirits raced to light up a way for him to get out through a hole. After that he supported his father even more circumspectly. Due to this, his mysterious virtue flourished, and he became the ruler of the land. This was a result of serving his parents well.

"When King Wen was crown prince, his great filial piety was such that every morning and evening he would go to the threshold of the royal chambers and ask the attendants how his parents were. When he was told they were fine, the crown prince would smile warmly. If they were a bit out of sorts, the face of the crown prince would be filled with anxiety. At mealtimes, the crown prince would unfailingly see that the food was neither cold nor too hot; in the course of meals he would unfailingly supervise the portions and then withdraw.

"If the attendants announced an illness, the crown prince would formally fast. The crown prince would respectfully examine their food and personally taste their drink. If the food tasted good to the king, the prince would also be able to eat; if the king tasted little of the food, the prince would not be able to eat to satiety. When the king recovered from illness, only then would the prince also revert to normal. If the queen mother made a mistake, the crown prince would admonish her in a pleasant tone of voice; he would always be respectful toward anyone or anything the queen liked, even her pets.

"Thus, filial piety perfected in himself, his Way spread through the land. A classic song says, 'The ascent and descent of King Wen was assisted by Nature in both calm and action, both advancement and retirement.' That is why the tyrant Chau was not able to assassinate him. He was informed by a dream how long he would live, and he divined a thirty-generation and seven-century reign for the dynasty he established, as decreed by Nature. This was a result of serving his parents well."

Min Tzu-ch'ien said, "Now that I have had the fortune of hearing about the logic of serving our parents well, may I ask about the principles of educating children?"

Confucius responded, "When the Three Kings educated their children, they always taught them etiquette and music. Music is a means of cultivating the interior, etiquette a means of cultivating the exterior. When etiquette and music are cultivated together, then the countenance of virtue shines in one's appearance, so one can be warm yet reverential, cultured and civilized.

"The vassal of another will even kill himself if it would benefit his lord; how much the more will he do what profits himself if it is good for his lord. Therefore, the kings selected people who were true and upright to establish as royal tutors for their children, wishing their children to know the ways proper to parents and children, rulers and subjects, the old and the young.

"Only after you know how to be a son can you become a father. Only after you know how to work for someone else can you become the director of others. Only after you know how to serve others can you employ others. These are the Three Kings' principles of educating children."

Min Tzu-ch'ien withdrew and put this into practice at home. After three years, no words were said causing division among members of the family. His associates praised his trustworthiness, his neighbors praised his humaneness, his clan praised his brotherliness; the fame of his virtuous behavior flooded the land. This was a result of serving his parents well.

The crown prince of Ch'i was sitting in an observatory tower. Chuang T'a, Lord of Yen, showed up in a tall hat, with a dignified appearance, wearing a jade-hilted sword in his belt at his left side, with a jade ornament hanging from his belt at his right side, so lustrous that the shine of the left lit up the right, and the shine of the right lit up the left.

The crown prince, reading a book, paid no attention to him.

The Lord of Yen asked, "Does the state of Ch'i have a treasure?"

The crown prince said, "The ruler is trustworthy, the ministers are loyal, and the farmers support the government. This is the treasure of Ch'i."

Hearing this, the Lord of Yen took off his sword and left.

AH, WELL! IF PEOPLE have biases and blind spots, they never get to know themselves. The wise view them with magnanimity and forgiveness, and do not criticize. Petty people talk too much out of contempt and attraction. Parents and relatives disagree in their sympathies and jealousies. When people have biases and blind spots, how do they not know themselves?

This is why cultured people examine themselves at all times to see if they have any faults. Wearing the appropriate clothing, eating the appropriate food, if they realize when they are at fault and are unable to correct it, cultured people consider this shameful.

When they want to say something but know it cannot be put into practice, cultured people seldom speak. When they are to criticize the evils of the hoi polloi, they look to see if they themselves are good. When they are to criticize the perversity of the hoi polloi, they look to see whether they themselves are upright. This is called introspective clarification.

THE SON OF MR. TI HSI was very dutiful and diligent. Ti Hsi cared for his son, but liked to fool him. Ti Hsi went out one morning and returned home at night to announce that so-and-so had died. His son believed him, even though that person was still alive. Another night, he announced that a certain individual had done him harm. His son went to get revenge, but found that no wrong had been done. Another night, he declared that such-and-such a person was ailing. His son went to see the patient, only to find that there was nothing wrong with him. It was like this every time.

As the years went on, Ti Hsi's son was certainly dutiful and diligent, but when it came to what his father told him, the son felt less and less confidence in what he heard from his father.

Eventually the people of the locality got sick and tired of Ti Hsi's misleading talk, and they plotted to kill him. Ti Hsi heard about this and ran home in fear to tell his son. His son did not really believe him, and so Ti Hsi got killed.

PEOPLE WHO TALK A LOT are called indiscreet, but there are also people of few words who do not keep secrets. Compulsive people are called unstable, but there are also those who are physically relaxed yet mentally excitable. Promiscuous people are called base, but there are also those who are outwardly pure while inwardly polluted. No end of similar examples could be cited: if not for penetrating perception, how can you find out the whole truth?

AT TIMES WHEN THERE are things to which one cannot but respond, even if inwardly still, one is outwardly active; it is easy to act and hard to be still. At times when there are things that one cannot but seek, one is inwardly pensive while outwardly expectant; after what is anticipated arrives, one is happy.

Therefore, those who are outwardly calm but inwardly astir damage their nature by activating thought. Those who race after profit injure their reputations by exerting efforts.

There may be things in human life that do not succeed as one wishes; in such circumstances, to announce that the time is not right is no different from accepting the death sentence and waiting to be executed. Is that not dangerous?

People of tremendous talent and comprehensive knowledge who have been employed should properly say it is not that the age is impure, but that destiny has not yet given the command; would that not be so?

Those who are skilled at criticism strive to preserve the essential nature of the persons they are addressing, while trimming and regulating that from which their feelings arise. Because of this, both sides make progress; they are friendly and respectful, earnest and serious.

Those who are not skilled at criticism strive to attack the essential nature of the persons they are addressing, yet are ignorant of the source of their feelings. Because of this, enmity and suspicion build up day after day.

What children choose is rejected by the elderly; what the ears and eyes enjoy is disliked by the intellect. Those who fiercely blame the ignorant of the world are themselves as yet unwise; those who fiercely blame the confused of the world are themselves as yet unenlightened. When the unwise criticize the ignorant masses, the unwise perish because of it. When the unenlightened criticize the confused masses, the unenlightened suffer because of it.

# THE WAY OF AGRICULTURE

IF PEOPLE ABANDON THE fundamental for the secondary, then there is disunity. Without unity, defense is impossible, and war is not feasible.

If people abandon the fundamental for the secondary, then their productivity will be limited. When productivity is limited, people easily drift into vagrancy. When people easily drift into vagrancy, the country suffers disasters from time to time, and everyone wants to emigrate, no longer wishing to live there.

When people abandon the fundamental for the secondary, then they crave knowledge; and when they crave knowledge, there is a lot of deceit. When there is a lot of deceit, then laws are artificially elaborated. When laws are artificially elaborated, then what is right is considered wrong, and what is wrong is considered right.

The means by which ancient sage kings governed people was by first striving to get people to farm. Getting people to farm is not just for the sake of amassing profits; what is valued is carrying out their aims.

When people farm, they are uncomplicated; when people

are uncomplicated, they are easy to employ. When people are easy to employ, the land is secure; when there is security, the leadership is respected.

When people farm, they are innocent; when they are innocent, they have few personal prejudices. When people have few personal prejudices, then fair common law is established, with deep and far-reaching power.

When people farm, their produce is abundant. When their produce is abundant, they do not drift into vagrancy. When they do not drift into vagrancy, they live out their lives where they are, without second thoughts, and the whole land is of one mind. Even the social order of ancient sage kings was not beyond unifying the hearts of all in the land.

The reason ancient sage leaders worked at plowing and spinning was to make these basic education. This is why emperors personally led the lords in plowing the sacred fields of the ancestral shrines, and the grandees had ranks according to their work; it was to encourage people to honor productivity. The empress and the concubines would lead the palace ladies in raising silkworms in the suburban mulberry groves and public fields as an instructive example for housewives.

Males do not weave, yet they wear clothes; females do not plow, yet they eat. Men and women exchange the fruits of their labor, helping each other do their work. This is the system of the sage kings.

Therefore they respected the seasons and loved the days; they measured their fruits to determine accomplishments. They did not stop working unless they were old, and did not take time off unless they were sick. One person working thus could feed ten people.

When they were engaged in seasonal work, they did not undertake major construction projects and did not equip armies. The men did not take wives from elsewhere, and the women did not go elsewhere to marry. The men did not go out riding, and the women did not take trips, because that would interfere with agriculture.

The Yellow Emperor said, "The four seasons cannot be corrected. We only correct the five grains." The one who sows and cultivates them is humanity; the one who creates them is Heaven; the one who nurtures them is Earth. Therefore the sowing requires feet, raking soil over newly sown grain requires a harrow, weeding requires hands. This is called the Way of tilling.

Agriculture takes care of food, crafts take care of utensils, commerce takes care of money and goods. If the seasonal work is not respected and is usurped by construction projects, this is called a great ill. When the sowing is too early, it is ahead of the season; if too late, it is behind the season. If cold and heat are irregular, the crops suffer many blights.

The earth produces growth fifty-seven days after the winter solstice; this is when the first plowing is done. The Way of agriculture is to sow the living when seeing life, and to reap the dead when seeing death.

Heaven creates the seasons and produces wealth without making promises to humankind. In years of abundance, honor the earth; in fruitless years, honor the earth. Do not miss human timing; act when the time is right, desist when the time has passed. Then the old and young can be fully aroused.

Those who do not know the timing of the seasons violate them before they have even arrived and long for them after they have gone; and right at the precise timing of the season, they slight it. This is the lowest way of going about the work.

Plowing should be done in dry weather, making the soil fertile and the earth warm. Crops like to germinate in soft soil and grow in firm earth. Be careful not to sow seed too thickly or too sparsely, and do not spread too little or too much soil over it. Irrigation channels should be deep and straight, and fields should be moistened evenly.

When there is yin (water) below and yang (sunlight) above, only then does everything grow. When seedlings are set out in rows, they grow quickly; because the strong and the weak do not encroach upon each other, they enlarge rapidly. Keep the rows straight, with space in between to let the air circulate. Then there will be a harvest, at a highly efficient rate of return on labor.

If crops look abundant from a distance but turn out to be sparse when you get up close, this means the soil is depleted. When ground grows wild when not weeded, but nothing grows after it has been weeded, that means the soil has been damaged by the way it has been treated.

When sprouts are young, they should be separate; when grown, they should be together; when ripe, they should support each other. Set them in groups of three, and the plants will produce much fruit.

Seedlings are affected negatively when they do not grow in unison and die in unison. This is what makes the first to grow produce fine grain, while that which grows later makes only empty husks. Therefore when you thin them out, you let the earlier ones grow and remove the later ones.

When planting on fertile ground, do not crowd seedlings; when planting in poor soil, do not isolate them. If you plant too thickly on fertile ground, there will be a lot of empty husks; if you plant too thinly on poor soil, many of the plants will die. Those who do not know how to cultivate will get rid of the earlier ones and nurture the later ones, with the result that they reap husk instead of grain.

When conditions above and below are unstable, much of the crop dies. Grain in good season has long stems, big stalks, round kernels, and thin husks. The grain is sweet and fragrant, easy to polish, and nutritious. Mistimed grain has long beards, small stalks, slender kernels, a lot of bran, and the fruits tend to fall off while still green.

Millet in good season has ears without long tassels; the grain can be removed by hand, and there is little bran. Mistimed millet has big roots, flowering stalks, big leaves, and short ears.

Rice in good season has large stalks with long joints and ears like horsetails. Mistimed rice has slender stalks and is not thick; it is poor and dies in the fields.

Hemp in good season has sparse nodes and is light in color; it has strong fibers and small roots. Mistimed hemp has many branches, short stems, enlarged nodes, and worm-eaten leaves.

Beans in good season have long stalks with short feet; their pods are clustered in double sevens; they have many branches, sparse nodes, luxuriant foliage and plenty of fruit, which weighs in heavy and is filling when eaten. Mistimed beans stretch out like creepers, with insubstantial foliage and weak roots, few nodes and small pods.

Wheat in good season has long stalks in clusters, with heads of double rows of seven, thin husks and tawny color; it is rich in calories and nutrition. Mistimed wheat is tubercular and sickly, with weak seedlings and excessive beards.

Therefore crops in good season are abundant, while mistimed crops are limited. The cereals are all good to eat accordingly; they strengthen people's limbs and make the ears and eyes clear and bright, so injurious energies do not get in, and the body suffers no cruel disasters.

Excellent indeed are the words of Confucius: "Eat enough in winter, and the body is warm; eat enough in summer, and the body is cool." When warmth and coolness are appropriate to the season, then people have no sickness or fever. When people have no sickness or fever, then epidemics do not go around. When epidemics do not go around, all can live out the years given by Heaven.

Therefore it is said that grain is the heaven of the people. This is why kings who prosper work at agriculture. If kings do not work at agriculture, they are abandoning the people. If kings abandon their people, what constitutes their countries?

# THE WAY OF WAR

WHEN KING CHING OF Ch'in was going to show his military strength to the world, he sent an emissary to fetch the Master of the Hidden Storehouse, to whom he offered fifteen conquered towns as an inducement.

When the Master of the Hidden Storehouse arrived, he was given lodging in the quarters reserved for important guests. King Ching was unable to ask him any questions for three days.

Taking a lower seat and humbly according fullest respect to the Master, the king said, "Has Heaven no intention of pitying me?"

The Master of the Hidden Storehouse serenely looked to the side and said, "I thought the king would ask something different. Why are you so distressed? Because of killing. Being pressed, I will go along with your wishes, so that you can find out how to do it correctly; but that does not mean it is right."

The king made a full prostration, rose and straightened his robe, then sat formally with bowed head and said, "Whatever Heaven commands."

The Master of the Hidden Storehouse looked up at the eaves and sighed, then lowered his face. With a somber mien, he said, "War has existed ever since humankind has existed. All wars come from human force. Forcefulness in humans is received from Heaven. Therefore war comes from above, and there is never a time when it is not in operation. The upper and lower classes, the old and the young, the wise and the foolish, are the same in this.

"When you look into the signs of war, they are in the mind. When there is anger at heart but it has not yet been expressed, this is war! Hateful looks and angry faces are war. Boastful words and shoving matches are war. Exaggerated contention and aggressive combat are war. These four are conflict, large and small.

"Even before Pao Kou [who opposed the Yellow Emperor in the twenty-fourth century B.C.E.], people actually took up pieces of wood and fought. The Yellow Emperor used water and fire. Kung Kung fomented disorder. The Five Emperors struggled with each other; one was deposed as another arose, with the victor taking charge of affairs.

"There are those who have died from ingesting drugs, but it is wrong to wish to ban all medicines because of that. There are those who have died sailing in boats, but it is wrong to forbid the use of boats because of that. There are those who have lost countries by waging war, but it is wrong to wish to ban all warfare because of that.

"Warfare cannot be dispensed with, any more than water and fire. Properly used, it produces good fortune; improperly used, it produces calamity. For this reason, anger and punishment cannot be done away with in the home, criminal and civil penalties cannot be done away with in the nation, and punitive expeditions cannot be done away with in the world.

"Ancient sage kings had militias of justice; they did not do away with warfare. When warfare is truly just, it is used to eliminate brutal rulers and rescue those in misery. People's joy is as that of devoted children seeing their kind parents, like starving prisoners getting delicious food—they run to it with a cry, like a powerful catapult shooting into a deep canyon.

"What determines victory or defeat should not be sought elsewhere; it is imperative to go back to people's feelings. Human feelings are such that they want to live and hate to die; they want glory and hate disgrace. When there is but one way to determine death or life, disgrace or glory, then the soldiers of the military forces can be made to be of one mind.

"Generally speaking, it is desirable to have many troops, and it is desirable that their hearts be united. When all the military forces are of one mind, then order can be made unopposed.

"The best militias of ancient times esteemed order. To

those whose order was strong, adversaries are weak; in the presence of those whose order was trustworthy, adversaries were humbled. First master the one, and you master the other.

"If you can really achieve this, then how could opponents even be worth beating? Whenever opponents approach, it is in search of profit; if all they will get by approaching is death, then they will consider it profitable to run away. Then there is no need to cross swords. This is what is called the best militia.

"Extravagance, cruelty, treachery, and deceit are opposites of just principles. These forces cannot both win; they are incompatible. Therefore when a just militia enters enemy territory, the people know they are being protected. When the militia come to the outskirts of cities, it does not trample the crops, does not loot the tombs, does not plunder the treasures, and does not burn the houses. Prisoners are treated with consideration and returned. People are given reliable promises. Thus the support of adversaries is taken away, good and bad are illustrated, and disharmony and harmony are demonstrated.

"If you are like this, and there are still those who are obstinately vicious, who are contemptuous, self-indulgent, and heedless, then you may even take military action against them. First you make the announcement that the coming of the militia is to get rid of the enemies of the people, to follow the Way of Heaven; therefore it conquers the country without slaughtering the people, only executing those who deserve to be executed.

"Then you nominate and select outstanding people, the wise and the good, to honor them with entitlements. Seeking out the orphaned and widowed, the sick and the elderly, you rescue them and come to their assistance. Opening up the treasuries and granaries, you do not keep the goods to yourself, but share them respectfully.

"Now if there is someone who is able to safeguard the life or to cause the death of a single human being, everyone in the world would strive to serve that person; since a just militia safeguards the lives of individual human beings many times over, why would people not like it?

"Therefore, when a just militia arrives, people of the neighboring countries join it like flowing water; the people of an oppressed country look to it in hope as if it were their parents. The further it travels, the more people it wins."

Before the speech was even ended, King Ching rose and bowed, saying, "Now that I have gotten to hear your teaching, my energy has filled the universe, my will knows where to go, and yet my mind is ever more reverential."